Generis

PUBLISHING

PARTICIPATION AND SOLIDARITY

Osvaldo Della Giustina

CIP a Camerei Naționale a Cărții

Osvaldo Della Giustina

Participation and Solidarity/Osvaldo Della Giustina – Generis Publishing, 2020 (Print on Demand). – 190 p.: fig., tab.

Tit. orig.: Participação & Solidariedade

ISBN: 978-9975-3348-4-6

316.42

G 60

Cover image: www.pixabay.com

Online orders: www.generis-publishing.com
Orders by email: info@generis-publishing.com

To Gregório and Elizabeth, my parents, who bequeathed me their wisdom.

> "Where is the wisdom we have lost in knowledge?
> Where is the knowledge we have lost in information?"
>
> (T.J. Elliot)

INTRODUCTION

To the French Edition and the third Brazilian Edition

The first Brazilian edition was published in 2004, the data and the events discussed in this book may at first glance seem obsolete. They would be so, obviously, if this book only addressed the issue in a circumstantial manner.

However, Participation and Solidarity, has as essential content and as an objective, the analysis of the process of change or transformation, through which the evolutionary process of history or civilization is going, and its perspectives, starting with the scientific revolution and technology whose consequences we are currently experiencing.

In this respect, the data and the events that are being analysed have only an instrumental function, or they constitute only the indicators that have made possible to get to the analyses and to justify the book's proposals.

What is important, though, it is the process, the analysis and the proposal, rather than the data or even the events.

In the evolution of events, we can only remember the immigration of mass sinking in the European continent, with terrorism threatening societies as developed and secure as they are, economic crises are multiplying and affecting even the most prosperous and developed economies, size systems that dominate and influence the world threatening the pluralism, the diversity of cultures, individual freedoms, in a new form of world totalitarianism; we can only remember the growing number of excluded people and the awareness of their exclusion, while wealth and well-being are concentrated on individuals, groups, societies and countries, dangerously distancing themselves from the rest of the world, a process whose result was recently denounced by the British NGO OXFAM, concluding that 1% of the population of the Planet holds 62% of the world's wealth, so that only 38% of the remaining wealth is shared by the majority represented by 99%; we can also recall, finally, the pollution of the Planet and the depletion of natural resources, global warming and the deterioration of the atmosphere, and ultimately, insecurity, loss of values and despair about the future. Where are we going?

It should, nonetheless, be remembered that at the same time, more and more events around the world are organized to promote peace and justice, including the respect for the diversity of cultures and human rights, for the preservation of nature and the environment; in addition, it should be remembered that the world is spreading the rejection of all forms of oppression, of the violence and oppression on individuals, as well as on regions, communities and peoples, races or any other attribute; that the respect for human rights is increasing in importance more and more for people around the world and that the highest respect is shown in a wide range of countries and that the world is dedicated to the preservation of the environment, of the resources of nature and the Earth which is increasingly seen as the common dwelling of men and therefore, of common responsibility and solidarity.

Participation and Solidarity focuses on the examination of the greatest event in history: the globalization pushed to the extreme by the continuous progress of the forms of communication, including virtualization, among other factors that has led the civilization almost to overcome the forms of space and time, a limit which, in addition to knowledge, has started to constitute the fundamental conditioning of the organization and human behaviour.

This new world has become incompatible with the concepts, the rules and processes that ordered the world in the past, the incompatibility which, if not reversed, will lead the process to some form of breakdown.

Therefore, it is important to know that the path to the new society is an irreversible path and it concerns the survival of civilization and the future of the human race.

The book is an invitation to those who are, or will be, dedicated to the analysis of this process, of people or institutions, so that they can join those who believe that only through science and technology, they will we be able to save the world from the break-up of civilization, that is to say, the advent of a participatory and supportive civilization can contribute to the safeguard and sustainability of the same civilization, or of mankind.

Those who understand this dimension beyond the conjuncture, they are part of the "Mass of Consciousness", a term coined in this book.

They should also have no doubt that the Mass of Consciousness and its values, by asking for change, will help to awaken the consciousness of the new civilization where the full human greatness and advances in science and technology will finally come together.

PARTICIPATION AND SOLIDARITY

The Third Millennium Revolution (II)

Explanatory note

1. THE MEANING OF THE PROPOSAL

Participation and solidarity x exclusion and conflict.

Participation and Solidarity are concepts that have recently shaped the consciousness and aspirations of humanity. Not only the aspirations, but also the practice or actions of millions of people and social groups around the world. This ever-growing phenomenon, which we will now call the mass of consciousness, will have to shape the future as an alternative for the survival of humanity - the inevitable and irreversible journey of the human species.

Why should social structures and institutions - economics, politics, relations between nations - going against this global consciousness or mass consciousness, continuing to be organized by selfishness, competition, concentration or accumulation, generating exclusion, insecurity and conflict?

Overcoming this contradiction is the extreme challenge posed by this transition of civilization from the industrial age, where we come from, to the post-technological age, where we are now arriving. It is not viable to maintain this contradiction between the tendency of history, or of human evolution, expressed in the mass of consciousness, and the fact that some people want to keep, using technological means, universities, world systems and opinion formers, which condition and manipulate the human mind and behaviour, threatening to impose on humanity the worst of totalitarianisms: a global dictatorship, represented by the castration of the capacity for critical analysis and alternative formulation on the part of people and cultures. Orwell was not completely right: the threat of a global dictatorship hanging over humanity is much worse than the one foreseen and announced, almost a hundred years before it happened - man dominated by the machine, ruthless eye to penetrate it without territorial, cultural, ideological, ethical and privacy limits.

Humanization of society - The revolution of the third millennium.

Some readers (of those who make up the mass of consciousness) of the book **Humanisation of Society - The Third Millennium Revolution**, which I published in 2001[1], at the dawn of this new era, the post-technological era, which has arrived as an imposition and requirement of technological progress, have found it difficult to identify among the graphs, figures and tables, the essence of the proposal it contains.

I therefore decided to take up the theme of that book again, limiting myself now to its essential content and leaving those who wish to plunge into figures and tables in order to demonstrate it, the patience to come back to it, apart from a few parts and a minimum of figures that I quote, which seemed to me sufficiently illustrative for the purposes of this book.

Thus, **PARTICIPATION AND SOLIDARITY** claims to go straight to the point, to the chain of ideas and concepts that forge this proposal.

This objective of restricting myself directly to the essential begins with the title of the book, which summarizes everything, although it may not please marketers and disobeys the dictatorship of the rules of success, which sees in the void of ideas and meaning, one of its sad – because of inhuman ways. PARTICIPATION AND SOLIDARITY sums up the ethical foundations of the post-technological society that must be made operational. The subtitle takes up the title of the previous *book The Revolution of the Third Millennium (II)*, in the certainty that there is no other means than this revolution to make viable the new civilization of the post-technological era, or the realization of the supreme vocation of the human species, including its survival, because of the dimension of power attained by technology.

More than a book to be marketed, therefore, **PARTICIPATION AND SOLIDARITY** is a book that must be thought and exploited.

---

[1] The Third Millennium Revolution - by Osvaldo Della Giustina - Ed. Litteris - R. Janeiro - 2001.

There are millions of people around the world who are looking for answers through reflection. They are also part of the mass of consciousness and are called upon to change the process and make change operational.

This is the essence of the process: to go from conflict, concentration and exclusion, to cooperation, deconcentration, solidarity and participation and thus to convergence or synthesis: to the humanized society, on the path of amortization to which Teilhard de Chardin refers to[2].

This path - of convergence, a vast expression, among men, of universal attraction - which governs the universe, is a general principle of nature, and cannot be different for the human species or for the realization of the nature of man, who is part of nature and its processes. In man, however, universal attraction, or convergence, takes on the dimension of love and freedom - because of consciousness.

The current orientations of human processes - however, still based on pre-potency, domination and conflict, i.e. on competition and concentration, which leads to exclusion, opposing the sense of convergence and love - integrate excessive imbalances into the necessary harmony of the process, and these excesses can lead human processes to break down, because the extreme imbalance in the whole of nature is unsustainable. And it cannot be different in human affairs.

But there's always time to redo, or rearrange trends.

Participation and Solidarity is a reflection on how to remake the trends so that, instead of the rupture, we finally continue on the path of sustainability of human processes - the balance and harmony of man with himself, with his environment and with the Universe, and this because the excessive power, or the dimension of things, that technology has put in his hands, no longer allows imbalance, at the risk of global rupture.

This, and only this, is the way to convergence, and therefore to love, or survival, at a time when man has discovered instruments capable of destroying the world and is using them, not only in the material sense, but in the broad and global,

---

[2] Chardin – Teilhard, O Fenômeno humano – AGIR, 1954

or civilizing sense. This is the direction to follow in order to build the post-technological civilization.

2. THE DEPHASING OF THE PROCESS

• The mass of consciousness.

PARTICIPATION AND SOLIDARITY, therefore, are feelings, aspirations and concepts that develop every day in the hearts and minds of individuals and peoples, but also in the way of acting of people and the many social organizations that bring them together.

The question is to make them operational in institutions - political, economic and social - in order to transform them into an instrument of change, to make institutions compatible with aspirations and with this awareness.

This transformation, which would make institutions conform to the consciousness of humanity in its evolutionary process, or to the mass of planetary consciousness, is a radical proposal. Radical in the sense that for participation and solidarity to become a practice of institutions and their relationships, it is necessary to promote change at the root. The change in forms of consciousness, concepts, social structures and human relations that, as a legacy of the past, still organize society and its relations. This change must reach the persons, peoples and nations, as well as the States that organize and represent them. The change seems, or indeed, must be very important, because very little, if anything, has changed in the principles governing the organization and functioning of society, as they were formulated before the great technological revolution arrived, starting in the middle of the last century.

However, it is necessary to stress out that this technological revolution has radically changed the conditions, circumstances and available instruments of human coexistence. Since the principles governing these processes have not been changed, dysrhythmia and imbalance have become inevitable, which have arisen as a threat to its continuity. It is because of this dysrhythmia and imbalance that change will have to be radical.

Electronics, fine chemistry, new physics, penetration into the nucleus of matter, the atom, genetic engineering and biology have precipitated, in a very short period of time, the emergence of a new world - globalization and change as a process, realities that retain little or no similarity, or relationship, to the world of the past.

On the other hand, the fundamental principles that continue to preside over the organization and human relations in this new reality of post-technological society remain the same as in the pre-technological era, the outdated times of the first Industrial Revolution: these fundamental principles boil down to competition and concentration as a means of domination and survival of the strongest, as in primitive nature, (without consciousness), excluding from the process the weakest competitors - or simply those who do not have the equivalent means of competition, concentration and competition. Brought to the post-technological era, these fundamental principles, in addition to exacerbating the process of exclusion of the weakest, or even the strongest, but less competitive, maintain in the field of ethics as presuppositions, the "ethical" principle of the "survival of the weakest" egoism, conflict, war, power and domination, i.e. they are opposed to universal aspirations, which are in the direction of the search for global equilibrium, the awareness of harmony, and therefore peace, participation, solidarity and love.

Either in the practical field or in the field of ethics - (concepts that are inseparable), these fundamental principles - selfishness, conflict, competition, concentration and exclusion that cause domination over one another - the old concepts of dominant and dominated, are not compatible with the world of dimension and speed that the new technology has introduced into the process. These aspects will be detailed in this book.

• The transition of civilization.

Transition of civilization, therefore, means that: referring to the foundations of social organization, it is not a proposal of surface, such as, for example, the third way, neo-socialism or neo-capitalism, or one of the different neo's that are fashionable, or in the media, without much critical analysis, applied as a Band-Aid on a deteriorating process.

In the context of the change of civilization we have arrived at, from the industrial, or pre-technological, era to the post-technological era, these expressions would be equivalent to speaking, in the context of other civilizational transitions, of neo-feudalism in the industrial era, or neo-tribalism, in the time of ancient empires, just to illustrate.

To realize that this moment in history constitutes a process of transition from a fundamental civilization to an understanding of what is happening in the world, as well as to grasp the meaning of this proposal.

They will not agree with this dimension, or will not understand it, those who are unable to free themselves from the concepts mentioned above, which also underlie the current organization of society and human coexistence, inherited from the pre-technological era. Neither will they understand this dimension, those who do not adhere to its concepts, the idea of process, or history, of time or space, conditioned that they are to numbers and quantities, and to immobile and stratified structures or simply to facts and conjunctures, as if reality is made up of facts and conjunctures and not processes[3].

---

[3]   At this stage, a warning is necessary to avoid the reductionist or simplistic approaches that experts make to any alternative ideas to their own orthodoxy and viewpoint and to interpret large and complex realities. I refer in particular to those who run society or the human process, as if it were summed up, or reduced to cash accounting, or to helping those who are excluded by the system.

This proposal does not call into question the need for currency stability, or financial balance in the overall process of change, just as it does not call into question the need for emergency programs, even of the size of the fight against hunger, the distribution of food baskets, or hunger-free Christmas campaigns, or the Happy Child and other similar initiatives, as long as they do not serve only to consolidate the status quo, or put consciences to sleep.

What is in question is whether these policies are sufficient to promote change, or rebalance the process.

In the first hypothesis specifically, the question is whether the path to a balanced cash balance can only be achieved through exorbitant interest rates and speculation on the financial market, in the context of the virtual, speculative economy, and, as they claim, this is the only alternative.

Obviously, it is not. There is a certain mental laziness in this posture, or a void of ideas, as Thomas Skidmore, the famous "Brazilian", calls it.

Achieving financial equilibrium could be made possible by the rational, economically sustainable use of the country's immense natural resources, in the case of Brazil, or of the Planet, potential resources often ignored, especially in excluded countries, by the very conditions of exclusion of the population and people. There are financial resources in the country and in the world, for this other way of generating balance, including financial, through policies and projects in favour of the Planet, the Country or the World.

In short, financial stability is necessary and important.

But in itself is insufficient and may consolidate the continuation of hunger and exclusion, as being at an increasing rate in Brazil and in the world - given that the financial issue is not an equation, as it is often called, but only a duration of the real equation which is man or society: it

Finally, they will not understand this proposal either, those who have not grasped the meaning of the concept of civilization, but reduce the concept of the human being, his conscience and his history, to profit, to the accumulation of everything and nothing and to the domination, or control of the world, or parts of it, which is reductionism in general with tragic consequences for the human species. They have not yet been able to realize the meaning of life, the gift of quality of life, the meaning of living and coexisting in the human dimension - the sense of the vocation of the human species, that the mass of consciousness is about to awaken and is spreading more and more, every day. For them, as for animals, so to speak, there is no meaning, or vocation, in the act of being and existing. Although, even for animals, as for all nature, there is meaning.

Despite this, transformation will occur as a requirement of the technology itself, or as an inevitable outcome for the survival of the human species. It is best if it occurs through the consciousness and will of man, in the light of the full perception of the process, on which he would concentrate his ethical consciousness, through the conformity of what is and what must be, namely the nature of each component of the process, in the stage, or state in which it is, and through the perception of how it must transform itself to remain faithful to its nature[4].

---

is a huge misunderstanding to want to settle the term to the detriment of the equation, as has been wished since then.

A similar reasoning applies to the issue of helping the excluded through emergency projects - the fight against hunger has been cited as an example. It is necessary. But if we do not question the model - and if we do not modify it - that produces exclusion and therefore hunger, we take water out of the tank - drops, while the taps always spout poverty, exclusion and hunger in double dimension compared to the hunger that we want to reset, the misery that we want to fight and the exclusion that we imagine eliminating.

[4]   This book starts from philosophical presuppositions, from philosophy conceived as a science of absolute methodological rigor, in order to identify the nature of phenomena and its functioning, unlike the limited understanding of those less accustomed to the use of this tool, who need this explanation.

Nature is not made of specialties.

Nature is made up of a set of specialties - and that is very different. These specialties are structured with each other in an interdependent way and play complementary and necessarily harmonic roles. Nature, therefore, as a whole, is a complex, bound by absolute osmosis, and is therefore an organism. Social nature is also an organism.

When a specialty takes the place of the whole or ignores it - it overturns the whole, the process, restructuring and breaking it.

Thus, when the economy takes the place of society as a whole (the term takes the place of the equation), tramples on ethics, distorts the law, disrupts society, and vice versa, i.e., when the part takes the place of the whole, it turns into fundamentalism, whether religious, cultural, economic or political, as is fashionable, threatening humanity.

This is why the civilizing transition means a radical change, because participation and solidarity - the ethical foundations of the post-technological age and the expression of the mass of consciousness - will not succeed as long as social order or organization is based on competition and concentration, now driven by the dimension and speed of technology. Precisely, to these bases of ethical dimension, it is necessary to give them new tools and operational mechanisms, capable of making the organization of society coherent with its aspirations or conscience.

• The threat of breakup.

The dimensions and consequences of maintaining dysrhythmia between, on the one hand, the levels reached by technology and, on the other, the principles that continue to organize (or disrupt) human coexistence must lead to the inevitable breakdown of the process; or the opposition between feelings, aspirations and the mass of consciousness in formation, within the framework of the current organization (order) that is maintained or imposed on humanity. Moreover, other ruptures have taken place in the past, but there is a difference between them and the rupture that now threatens the process.

In the past, ruptures were localized in space and diluted in time, over millennia or centuries. The present rupture, if it occurs, taking into account the

---

For this reason, the science of the specialty must exist, but it must subordinate itself to the science of the totality or integrate with it. Each specialty must identify its complementarities, its interdependencies, as an indispensable means to build the harmony and viability of the parts.

At the major root of this science of the nature of things and processes, there is philosophy, as a science and not only as a practice, as a definite methodological science that seeks to identify the nature and interactions of the parts that make up the complexity of the whole.

This book, or this interpretation and proposal for the structuring and functioning of society, in the state in which history has arrived, or human evolution, the stage of the post-technological era, is based on the nature of things and processes and the process of evolution of man and things.

The analysis of specialties is merely the verification of their identities with nature, or of their disruptions, and the definition of ways to maximize their complementarity and harmonious interdependence.

This is the only way to find ways to make the process viable. I know that some people prefer to think of the process as conflict (or war), conditioning and power (dictatorship), or simply disorder (chaos) and competition (survival of the fittest). They cite the past in their defense. I oppose them to the evolution of the process and its conscious component - man. I oppose them the present and the technological leap I oppose them the future - the destiny and vocation of the human species.

characteristics and the dimension of the technology that generates it, will be, or could be, instantaneous and global.

This is an essential consideration, which makes the current threat totally different from the past, with unimaginable consequences for the future.

I would not say that, as examples or signs of the advent, or characteristics of this rupture, one could propose considerations around the attack that destroyed the towers of the New York World Trade, or the attack on the Pentagon or, for some, the White House, the symbols and headquarters of the apparent world power and the basic pillars that support the current organization. Nor would I say that they would be signs, the reactions, at the same level and with the same concepts of the American President George Bush - czar of the last of the empires, when he declared against terror, the terror of war, or if you like, a Manichean vision, already condemned at the beginning of the Middle Ages, dividing the peoples between the good and the bad, the bandits and the good guys, as in the westerns, which must occupy the cultural memory of his adolescence, inspiring his thirst for power to control the world and history. All the last emperors in history have thought and acted in the same way, and have always been the last.

However, blind to the lessons of history, the current system will maintain or will try to maintain control of the process until it breaks down, if the mass of consciousness, rationalized in a joint creative effort to generate the new civilization, fails to reverse the process in time.

Signs of rupture, however, precede the episode of September 11, 2002 - which opened the third millennium. These signals are in the nearly 3 billion people excluded from the benefits and wealth offered by technology, many of whom do not even have access to the fundamental rights to eat their fill, to be healthy and to live. This fact becomes all the more serious when we know that, if this current model of concentration and exclusion continues, this number could double in the coming decades. The signs of rupture are also present in the destruction of the planet's natural resources and the rapid degradation of its ecological balance; they are, above all, in the offended human consciousness, whose mass is growing until, in a certain way, the fracture of the balance takes place, and the rupture will be inevitable.

It doesn't matter how the breakup can happen, and that's not the point of this book of the imagination. That's the role of novels, fictional films or dilettantes of futurology exercises. But we are running towards rupture, if we are unable to reverse the process, by putting man at another level or stage of his history, or of the history of his evolution. Moreover, for those who interpret it in this way, the disruption of the balance or the breakdown of the process may produce the synthesis of opposites now in conflict: those who concentrate and the excluded, the dominant and the dominated, the rich and the poor, the people, the inhabitants of the earth, or simply people.

However, this is not the hypothesis defended in this book because the question is whether there will be time or conditions for synthesis, given the size and speed of the process and the gaps that accumulate. The truth is that the synthesis could be anteceded by the putting into operation of the mass aspirations of the world consciousness, or by the will of man, and not simply as a result of the dialectic of history.

3. THE METHODOLOGICAL ISSUE

It can be assumed, however, that not only technology has evolved, or that evolution is an attribute applicable only to things. In reality, at the end of the evolutionary process is, or should be, man. It can also be assumed, and therefore, that man has evolved, or can evolve, more than things and is able to promote change - overcoming time, conflict and avoiding rupture or explosion. It is possible, according to this perspective, that man's consciousness goes beyond the dialectic of things.

That is the meaning and the *raison d'être* of this proposal. Of course, it opposes the "status quo" and disturbs those who benefit from maintaining the current "status" and all those who refuse to think alternatively, whether out of fear or because "thinking hurts", in Fernando Pessoa's poetic perception.

In addition to these reasons, there is the resistance of the owners of the systems and their power to limit the spaces essential to the debate of any alternative proposal, in the media or in predominant or accommodated circles, including academia, which often refuse to think. The spaces for reflection and debate may be small, and there will be no lack of arguments to make them even smaller, because arguments, if there are none, are made, La Fontaine teaches us in his reflections on the relationship between the wolf and the lamb - between the strongest and the weakest.

Some will also say that the proposal mixes sociology, politics, economics, psychology, ethics and even religion, or at least mysticism or metaphysics.

The statement is true, in the words. It is true to the extent that reality is also made up of this mixture. Any analysis that does not "mix" or consider all the components of reality is partial. What is necessary, however, is that the "mixture" does not escape the scientific method, which makes it possible to separate the components and organize them later. So there is the moment to separate things, as a method, and the moment to "mix" them, as a synthesis, or result. The Reality is not partial, segmented, as it is usually treated by specialists, nor is it merely a sum or juxtaposition of segmented parts. Economists consider the economy as if it were society and want to construct reality according to this presupposition. Sociologists, philosophers, politicians, psychologists, mystics or saints adopt a similar attitude, with the same frequency; the saints too, why not? This is the unscientific tendency to transform the term into an equation.

When these perspectives are not brought together to form a synthesis - the "mixed" reality - the essence of what has been called a holistic vision, the reality we arrive at can become, or indeed does become, altered, dissonant - conflictual; the various points of view become mutually exclusive; society, or human conviviality, tends to disintegrate, to enter into chaos, or into conflict. All this indicates that this is happening at the origin of the crises that affect the process; and thus at the root of the uncertainties and quests, or perplexities about the future of humanity, or of its parts. This is because the synthesis - or the ordered "mixing" of reality is missing.

So it is not the proposal that mixes everything up. The reality is "blended", harmoniously "blended". And, woe to those proposals which, considering the reality as a whole, or in the whole of its parts, are not capable of promoting synthesis, or harmony, even if the proposals are not specialized in each part.

The current model of organization and functioning of society and its institutions is not capable of such harmonization, since the apparent precision of each part is achieved at the expense of the exclusion and lack of harmony of all these components.

Thus, ethics, like politics, economics, relations and human coexistence, which, by presenting their specialized models as if they were the whole, provoke discord in the orchestra, even if they play well on their own instrument.

Despite of these threats, the discussion about new perspectives should prevail in the universities - supposed to be centers of analytical and synthetic thought, capable of generating innovation; in the churches, too, by hypothesis, consciousness of society; among political leaders, who, because of their function, are able to perceive the moment, capable to grasp the meaning and aspirations, to establish or to institutionalize change, above the small and immediate interests that inspire the action of a few; above all it will prevail among communicators, with the immense power they have to manipulate the means of communication.

It is in the hands of these people, or those who have a global vision of society and its processes, that the alternative of change is to be found. I have reasonable expectations that the debate will open the doors of the communication media, the media, the churches, the universities, and that it will lead to changes in the proposal for action that has now been established.

4. THE ORIGINS OF THE PROPOSAL

The proposal for "**PARTICIPATION AND SOLIDARITY**" did not come on its own. It arose from dozens of moments of learning, reading, access to communication, listening to people, dozens, hundreds of people, and in universities, in congresses, in the media. It was born from seminars, conferences and reflections, in the long learning of life, in the daily reflection, in dialogue and debate. Truth is everywhere, and, therefore, it is a long way to find it, to rationalize it and to put it to the debate, to prove its coherence.

Originally, this proposal to organize society began to take shape more than 20 years ago, when the book was published around this theme: **THE AGE OF MAN - The Foundations for a New Social Order**[5], based entirely on principles compatible with the changes brought about by the technological revolution,

---

[5] By the author - A Idade do Homem - Ed. Almed, São Paulo, 1982.

deconcentration and cooperation, or universal ethical consciousness - participation and solidarity. The initial conception has slowly improved, through successive works, seeking forms and offering debates, many debates which, in disagreement and agreement, have made it evolve.

In the past, ideas were born and took shape from the philosophy course begun at the Viamão seminar and completed at the PUC, both at the Rio Grande do Sul, with active participation in political life and student life; then, in the state of Santa Catarina, especially in the conception and direction, for 13 years, of the Educational Foundation of the South of Santa Catarina, FESSC today University of the South of Santa Catarina - UNISUL, in the courses given there, in contact with young people, students, teachers and professors in the direction of an institution that was - and is - of a great human dimension.

I especially emphasize what I wrote in the Constitutional Proposal for a New Society, in 1987[6], and in Reflections on Education[7], in 1989, in its introductory part.

In 2001, I published **Humanisation of Society: THE REVOLUTION.** This book has consolidated the long evolutionary process of interpreting the human process and life in society, synthesized and complementary, now in **PARTICIPATION AND SOLIDARITY, The Third Millennium Revolution (II).**

I hope that this long sought-after or constructed synthesis can definitively consolidate the proposal, not only because of the debates we have had, through the multiplied experience and continuous reflection, but above all because of the evolution of the process taking place in the world at the end of this century and the beginning of the millennium. **This evolution confirms the tendencies denounced in the last 20 years, which indicates, exactly for this reason, the urgency and the need for everyone, each in his or her own space, to study the civilizing process and to contribute to it. The analysis, the numbers are there, in "The Third Millennium Revolution"[8], and some of the numbers and their analyses have been transcribed, because the evolution of the process and the debarments mentioned have simply validated them.**

---

[6] idem Constitutional Proposal for a New Company - Open Market, Porto Alegre, 1987.
[7] idem - Reflections on education - UFSC Publisher, Florianópolis, 1989.
[8] de l'Auteur - La Révolution du Troisième Millénaire, Ed. Litteris, Rio de Janeiro, 2001.

In **Participation and Solidarity - The Third Millennium Revolution (II)**, emphasis is placed on the assertion that this revolution is yet to come, and that is why the title is repeated there. The text wants to continue to bring together more consciences, other proposals and all those who unite the aspirations and the desire to build an alternative world towards the future; a civilization adequate to the process of evolution that has brought us to the post-technological era - the new millennium: a human, participatory and supportive world, different from the world that threatens us.

After all, it is love (attraction and complementarity, not repulsion or conflict) that moves the sun and all the stars - according to Dante Alighieri's poetic perception. Why wouldn't love also have the capacity to move the human species, man being the conscience of the Planet and, who knows, of the Universe?

Osvaldo Della Giustina
Brasília, 2004. 31

PART I

THE ESSENTIAL NATURE OF HUMAN PROCESSES

1. THE ANTHROPOLOGICAL VIEW

1.1 – THE EVOLVING PROCESS: COMPLEXIFICATION AND FREEDOM.

• Any evolution is a process that starts from the simple to the complex.

This path, as Teilhard de Chardin already taught, was dedicated to the study of man and his origins, in his essential work - The Human Phenomenon, completed in 1940 and published posthumously in 1951.

From this principle, we deduce that the more complex a being is, the higher he is on the scale of evolution. This happens with all the components of this scale, at the physical, biological, psychological or spiritual level. In reality, as the process of complexification takes place, the being comes closer to the multiplicity of functions, relationships, organization and, consequently, to greater fullness, or perfection.

This path to perfection, however, will only occur on the condition that, at the same time, the organization of complexity occurs. If this parallel organization does not occur, the growth of complexity leads to chaos. Chaos, i.e., the disorganization of the components of being, means the negation of the harmonious functioning of the whole, or of the complementarity of the parts, and thus death. Some admit (perhaps well) that death or chaos is the condition, or the restarting of life. But it does not seem to be a necessary path or passage.

The organization of complexity occurs in inanimate beings, of very primitive form, because they are of minimal complexity. In living beings, this organization begins to be more complex. The growth of complexity provokes a certain form of relationship, or vital impulse, turned towards its own organization and therefore towards the preservation of life. Life, which flows from this organization, constitutes a higher echelon than a simple physical or mechanical organization.

23

This vital impulse can be called instinct, because it is not yet a conscious phenomenon, sufficiently complex and, therefore, free. For this too, it is repetitive and necessary, and in order not to admit several solutions or options in its forms of relationship, or reaction, it is not free. Not being free, it is not characterized as a conscious act, or human, but only physiological, in the field of biology, or physiology, to whom it is up to explain it.

In man, to the physical, or mechanical organization of nature and instinct, or physiological reasons, is added consciousness, or all the faculties that are part of it - intelligence, perception, feeling, emotion, which make the process of organizing complexity a free process. Therefore, the same cause does not necessarily produce the same effect, but admits a variety of solutions, due to the complexity and the action of the consciousness exerted on it, which allows alternative choices. The human process becomes, therefore, a free process, since it is complex and conscious.

Thus, from this process, it follows that the more complex a being is, the greater the number of elements, or alternatives, or facets of each element that can be juxtaposed or ordered differently. This principle is valid as much for the organic, psychological, social elements, as for the conceptual elements. We can therefore say that the more complex the being is, the freer he is, or the more conditions he has for the exercise of his freedom, because of the consciousness that acts on diversity. We can also say that, conceived in this way, freedom becomes research, aspiration, goal or object of the evolutionary process. Everything that is simplified, standardized, unique, is opposed to freedom. The search for ordered complexity thus becomes the vocation of man, of him and of the whole evolutionary process, in which the whole of nature participates. On the other hand, everything that goes against complexity, goes against nature.

In short: freedom does not exist in the field of physics; it depends on instinct in the field of living beings, and is only realized in the realm of the human body - because of the extreme complexity and consciousness acting on complexity. There is, therefore, an ethical dimension, because of choices, related to the essence of the human process. As well as in the process of building society, or civilization, as a human construction.

• All evolution is, therefore, a path to freedom.

It can also be said, therefore, that just as the path of evolution is the path of complexity, the path of evolution is also the path of building freedom. The corollary of this is that everything that simplifies complexity, everything that unifies and standardizes, is a backward step in the evolutionary process, which limits the dimensions of freedom.

This essential understanding retains a parallelism with the anthropological vision of Teilhard de Chardin - I return to the French anthropologist who for decades devoted himself to the study of human evolution in its origins. Teilhard de Chardin represents the process of evolution like an arrow that, launched at the beginning of the Alpha point, seeks the Omega point, of fullness.

The primitive Alpha point is characterized by disorganization and therefore chaos or discord and violence. The Omega Point, where the realisation of the whole being is found, is identified by harmony, balance, attraction and harmonic awareness of the parts and therefore solidarity, peace or love. In this sense, on the path of the arrow, like the figurative Chardin, lies the essential anthropological concept - **the line of amortisation of the world. Neither peace nor love, in this sense, are confused with calm or immobility, but they constitute the own dynamic of the process that flows in accordance with its nature, and therefore with less stumbling, greater efficiency and better results.**

This anthropological vision is somehow related to the anthropocentric, or God-centred, viewpoint of theologians or sacred books: **"all things were made for man, and man for God,"** according to St. Augustine[9]... God, the essential love and therefore the Creator of all things - **"Love tends to spread"** - to create and procreate - **"love difusivum sui"**[10] by St. Thomas Aquinas - or **"love that makes the sun and all the stars move forward"**[11] , by Dante Alighieri.

Moreover, there is also a parallel between this philosophical or mystical principle and the principles of physics or biology, universal attraction or organic harmony. All nature functions by the attractive force of complementarity or

---

[9] Sto Agostinho, Bishop of Hipona - Confessions, sec. IV DC.
[10] Sto. Tomaz de Aquino - Theological short, sec. XIII.
[11] Alighieri, Dante - The Divine Comedy, sec. XVI .

convergence, not conflict or repulsion. Why should humans and human phenomena - the organization of society, function through discord, conflict, repulsion?

It is impossible to escape from this essential imperative of history or nature, whatever the faith, the mystical point of view, or the progress of science - of nature and of man. The facts of the technological age - the post-technological world generated by technology, show us that man, in his way of organizing himself, acting and coexisting, will have to insert himself in harmony with the Universe, in order to survive, and not only as an ethical imperative. If not, the human species will move, rapidly, towards some form of global rupture, frustrating or interrupting the process, for opposing nature, its own nature, the nature of its environment, or of the Universe, of which it is a part, the conscious part.

• The context in which it is possible to build society.

It is in this context that the evolution of society in its organization and in the relationship of its constituent elements - individuals, groups, cultures, nations, states and the whole network of relationships - should be examined. As in the overall process of nature, social organization and its relationships also move from the simple to the complex, from simple structures to structures and social relationships that become more and more complex. Yet it is this process that technological advances have made faster and more global.

Wrongly, however, systems tend to simplify and standardize structures, relationships and behaviours. In reality, the nature of the process - the continual increase in social structures and relationships - requires an equivalent, continuous and effective effort to reorganize society and its relationships, that is, the reorganization of the multiple and growing elements that make up the social structure (individuals, groups, cultures, nations and states) and their relationships, so that social life remains harmonious within the pluralism that comes from complexity. It is this pluralism, growing pluralism, which is the prerequisite for the exercise of freedom, and therefore the vocation of the evolutionary process, or of nature, which finds its fullest expression in man - because of conscience - and which, for this reason, must order the process in a harmonious and balanced way, in order to survive, because of the dimension of technology.

The effectiveness of this effort should lead to the post-technological society, to the new civilization with which we should enter the Third Millennium, minimally or maximally balanced, where harmony reigns over conflict (peace over war); love and freedom (solidarity and participation) over the instinct of greed and concentration (domination and exclusion). This change - or the advent of this new society brought about as an imposition of technology - is the condition for the survival of the process.

This is the path to the new civilization.

In this way, man will be progressively integrated into the harmony of the universe, being part of universal nature, just as society as a whole will be well inserted, as an expression of man's awareness of the environment in which he lives, his circumstances, according to Ortega y Gasset.

If this integration does not occur, chaos will prevail, and chaos will mean the break-up of the process, the frustration of nature - death, even if there is rebirth afterwards. But death could be avoided.

In summary, we can conclude:

1. that society, as an extension of man and an expression of nature, evolves like any process, from the simplest forms to the most complex forms of organization and relationship. Because of freedom, because of his capacity to create solutions, it is necessary that man can be the author - and the actor - of this construction;

2. that this construction implies a continuous work of reorganization of social structures and relations. When this does not happen, or if it does not happen, it generates the disturbances and crises resulting from structural imbalance - the dysrhythmia of the process, the conflicts and disturbances of social life, the path to chaos, or to the rupture we have been talking about;

3. that this continuous work should lead society to evolve from less human forms (because they are simpler and more conflictual forms of organization) to forms that are more in keeping with the vocation of man, nature and the whole process of evolution, that is, from simple forms of organization to more complex and orderly, and therefore more harmonious, cooperative and participatory - free forms. **This process can**

also be called the path of freedom, or the amortization of the world, a way of overcoming conflict, rupture, and chaos, replacing it with structural balance[12] - the path of security and peace.

The task requires an integral or holistic view of the world, the environment in which man lives and an extension of it, or of which man himself is a part - the conscious part. Building society, integrating himself into the nature that surrounds him, into the universe of which he is a part, man will build and preserve a part of himself.

I believe that there is no other interpretation that can be attributed to Ortega y Gasset, when he teaches that man is himself and his circumstances: I am We - that would not be a paradox; I am me, and the others (other things) are the others - that would indeed be a paradox.

Such a harmonic construction, each time it has not occurred in history, has determined the rupture as a consequence, which has cost society a great deal in terms of pain, suffering and delay in the process. This, contrary to the assertions of those who attribute to crises the advance of history, in a convenient and simplistic perspective. History has not progressed because of crises, which only reveal man's inability to prevent and avoid them. Man would have progressed further without them. Or he progressed despite the crises. The question is more serious today, because for the first time in history the price of this crisis can be instantaneous, absolute and global, because of the dimension of technology and the absolute and global power that it has generated and placed in the hands of men. It would be too much to ask, not only because of this threat, but because of the evolution of the human being in the evolution of all things, including technology, that the same mistakes are not made again, and that man be able to avoid crises and breakdowns, preventing them, preventing them from happening, and building his own future? Or will he simply know only to repeat the past?

---

[12] Human Rights and State Security - Revista Defesa Nacional - 1939

2. PROCESS DYSRHYTHMIA

2.1. - A PATENTED INTERPRETATION OF HISTORY

The answers to this question - whether man will be able to build his own future, or whether he will simply dwell on the past - are absolutely uncertain at the moment.

But, of course, if the elements that interact in the process of the evolution of beings, or of history, do not evolve in harmony, the result causes - as we have already said - a dysrhythmia in the process, and this dysrhythmia increases the threats of chaos, or rupture. These threats manifest themselves in the different crises, in their different forms, intensities and consequences.

At the end of the 20th century and the beginning of the millennium, this dysrhythmia is here. Things brought about by technology have got ahead of the evolution of man and his social organization, or his forms of coexistence.

It is stated in the book "The Third Millennium Revolution" that the price to be paid for overcoming this dysrhythmia, which generates crises, is always proportional to the time it takes to find the way to overcome the dysrhythmia, or crises, and therefore also proportional to the size of the distortions that this time allows to be introduced into the process.

• The nature of the crises.

There are moments in history when it is necessary to understand the crisis in this way: as components of the dysrhythmia introduced in the structural evolution of the process and not only as superficial crises or a situation of possible dysfunction of the conjuncture. We are living one of these moments.

Crises, when they arise from the dysrhythmia of the process, are essential, civilizational crises impose radical changes, because only the radical nature of the change is able to harmonize the process again. This new harmonization is a leap of civilization, capable of generating new forms of social organization, which history characterizes as ages, eras or civilizations, replacing organizational forms previously consolidated for centuries or millennia, which seemed definitive in the eyes of their contemporaries, but which were, in truth, already exhausted in its foundations due to evolution or changes in reality. Any change in civilization produces innovative forms of social organization in its foundations, structures and relationships. Thus, urban society was different from tribal societies; feudal society was different from the society of ancient empires, or the power of cities over the known world, as was the case with Babylon, Athens or Rome; industrial society was different from feudal society, kings, marquis, counts and barons, with their castles and privileges, and, around them, the serfs - the outcasts of the time.

The industrial era - the one that generated the foundations and forms of organization and relationships of the society in which we live - competition and concentration - was defined and conditioned by the evolution of science, which led to great discoveries and the invention of the steam engine, first a simple form of technology but a precursor of technological progress. However, scientific development, new discoveries and the steam engine were enough to generate the capital and a whole new form of social organization, no longer around castles, or lords, but around capital and the bourgeoisie which accumulated it. It also gave rise to new technologies - electronics, the atom, genes, fine chemicals, new physics, bioengineering. These new technologies, because of their size, have kept little relation to the original technologies, except for their origin. The changes resulting from the new technologies have launched history of humanity into a new era, which can be called post-technological, and which is, and will be increasingly different from the industrial society, generated by the steam engine technology, and its immediate consequences. However, the change of civilization has not yet taken place, or the transformation of society, its structures and the relationships and fundamental principles that should organize and direct it. The dysrhythmia between the change of civilization and the technological level that humanity has reached stems from this discrepancy.

As things have changed, driven by new technologies, in a dimension never seen before in history, man and the organization of the environment in which he lives - society, its structure, its relationships and relations with nature, or with its environment, and all the rules that govern them - have evolved very little, or not enough, and in many cases have not evolved at all, in the same way that the way of being and thinking of those who have in their hands the power to command or influence processes has not evolved. We could cite the case of governors and so many other leaders who, working in global systems - be they political, economic, financial, information or other - accommodate the world we live in and oppose change.

They like the institutions and systems they govern, or where they operate, continue to support the same foundations, rules and procedures generated in the context and procedures of the industrial era, or the first technological revolution - the steam engine revolution, which, at most, we could call the technological or industrial era. By way of example, we can consider the context and the constraints that existed in the mid-nineteenth century and that generated the socialist and capitalist theories - of Marx or Adam Smith, with no great differences in the practice of concentrating capital in the hands of the state, or in the hands of individuals or groups, depending on which one or the other - and that will continue to be supported on both sides by those who survive and want to maintain them, in a totally different historical context.

Thus, in the light of these old theories - from the time of the steam engine - it is claimed to organize and operate the post-technological society, global systems of information technology and the manipulation of life.

As a result, it is gaining in strength, the expression of a popular song: "**Even though we have done everything we have done, we are still the same and we still live like our parents**", an expression which in this context can also be linked to the bases of social organization, and not only to possible customs, usages or practices.

However, in spite of those who resist and their systems used to put consciences to sleep, the conscience of society - an irreversible expression of the nature and vocation of the human species, and an expression of feelings as well, of individual perception and consciences in favour of the harmony (of peace), solidarity (of love), and justice (of participation) - returns to the surface and will always be able to prevail over systems, overcoming dysrhythmia and inspiring and shaping civilization in the post-technological age. History shows that there is no way to prevent change, but it has also shown that change does not usually occur through the actions of the strongest, whose interests prevail, or the systems that benefit them. As in the past, however, no matter how great the power or interests of the strongest, as powerful as the Egyptian pharaohs, the Roman emperors, the kings of France, or the tsars of Russia, the owners of the existing empires, maybe, it is not enough to prevent change, but it has also shown that change does not usually occur through the action of the strongest, for whom the defense of their interests prevails, or of the systems that benefit countries or systems, the new empires will not be able to stop the process, command history or impose a straitjacket, so that change does not happen, or if it does happen, it bends to their interests. It would be better for themselves and for history, if the context, or the moment of evolution that we are living through, were to unite this time in favour of the change, opening their eyes to the fact that, in the post-technological era, it is no longer possible to repeat the past, cloak and dagger, or brandishing the muzzle of the animal, even if that muzzle is called a missile or nuclear warhead, or whatever apocalyptic expression may be displayed.

The revolution will take place in any case, with the owners of the systems, without them, or against them, if they stubbornly wanted to stop the process, that would be regrettable.

The inevitability of change begins with the perception that the maintenance of absolute power has become illusory, all the more so today than, or more so than, in the past. When the same technology, used by those in power, allows the destruction of the world to be encapsulated in a light bulb, hidden in a pocket, or subordinated to the push of a button, or to the access to the code that triggers the button, it is illusory to think of keeping control of the world and directing global processes indefinitely, especially when this control goes against the course of history, or is confronted with the mass of consciousness that, despite the systems, is growing irreversibly, among the excluded and among those who have not been dehumanized by power and wealth. They also unite for change.

• **Revolution does not mean violence.**

To say that we are living through a transition of civilization means that there is not enough correction or potential for correction for the distortions that affect the world or the country - Brazil or any other country in this interdependent world. The necessary revolution, which must be made at the beginning of this millennium, therefore needs urgency and sufficient depth to produce the leap that can bridge the gap between the industrial or pre-technological era and the post-technological era. This leap, or a change of civilization, means a major, wider and more radical as was the transition from feudalism to the industrial age, or from tribal life to urban organization, or from ancient empires - or from these to feudal civilization. It is this understanding that is necessary, as a kind of initial consensus, in order to successfully take up the challenge of this moment to make the new Millennium Revolution.

Speaking of revolution, therefore, does not at all mean the promotion of change through violence, armed conflict, war or terror, or other forms of violence proposed or practiced. The assumption of violence is a misconception of revolution. Because of this misconception, society has paid a very high price for making the necessary changes, i.e. radical or civilizational changes. Real revolution refers to the extent of the changes, not the form or method of making them.

The method of violence would not have been necessary in the past, it is even less necessary or acceptable in the present, because the capacity for violence has taken on a global dimension, which it has never had in the past.

In this context, the instruments of violence have also become globalized, like other things, exceeding all limits and escaping all forms of control, contrary to what those who think that globalization is only about power - or wealth, or the finances that support power - can deceptively imagine. What is happening is that, when globalized, the instruments of violence are accessible to everyone, and increasingly within anyone's reach. We have reached a point or a crossroads, where the owners of world power have in their hands the power to destroy the world, not only physically, but economically, socially, culturally, that is to say, to destroy civilization, and that is terrible. And not only them. Anyone who wants to do so and organizes himself to do so, including the so-called terror, can bring about this destruction, as can the terror of those who promote war, two sides of the same madness, or the same fundamentalism. Or simple resistance to change can also do this, cause a rupture.

According to this conception, and in this scenario, therefore, violence or transformation through violence, is an obsolete concept or strategy that could ultimately be acceptable and possibly even effective in the era of the steam engine; the helmet, breastplate and sword; the arrow and catapult; the slingshot, bow and arrow or muzzle of the animal. But transformation by violence is ineffective and suicidal when it is carried into the age of technology, or post-technology, global weapons, absolute systems, and retaliatory instruments increasingly within the reach of anyone who is determined to obtain them in any way.

But it is also for this reason - and not only because of the stage reached in universal evolution - that it is necessary that the revolution of the post-technological era be brought about by a new consciousness, which is also globalized, and by the essential capacity to, using one's own technology and the means it offers, modify the process and build the society adequate to the technological leap and the world that has emerged from it.

Would it be unreasonable to expect a human being in this new, post-technological world to be able to make this leap? Would it make more sense to use technology only to serve things, and destroy man, or civilization, to serve only profit and speculation, hard currency or concentrated power and wealth, excluding from the process a growing number of countries and human beings - the new colonialism of the post-technological age? After all, this is the most effective way to consolidate the dysrhythmia of the process, promoting imbalance, and therefore insecurity and the threat of collapse.

• The human species survives civilizational changes.

In reality, it is through changes in the civilization that history, or the human species, survives. I come back **to the Revolution of the Third Millennium** - the book quoted above. In this book, we can see that talking about changes in civilization, covering all forms of organization and functioning of society, may seem strange to some people. However, the change of civilization is an integral part of history, an imperative in the process of human evolution. Why shouldn't it happen when technology, more than the discovery of the use of fire, or the steam engine, has transformed things to a level never seen in past centuries?

"When man discovered iron, copper, bronze, and turned these metals into metallic weapons, he gained a minimum of control over nature and over other men, those who had no access to this innovation, let's say to this technology. This allowed him to replace the tribal regime with the first corporate organization - the city, superimposed on the tribe, or clan. In this way, the concepts of nation, people and government were born. The organization of empires, in a second phase, already more complex, extended and consolidated a new form of power and social organization that can perfectly characterize the first change of civilization. »

However, the caveman, or tribal man, never imagined that this was possible, and that there could be other forms of life than the one he had been used to living for generations, since the oldest traditions:

"When, millennia later, world empires - the globalization of the time, were overthrown under the influence of new realities - the increase in consciousness of being, the development of ancient science and philosophy in the West, the influence of Christianity, assumed by peoples thirsting for space and tired of servitude, the empires were fragmented, and power was divided. Then came feudal organization, which took similar forms in the Middle East of the grain viziers, or in the Far East of the samurai. A new civilization, a new conception of life, a new form of social organization, new instruments and different values dominated the world. »

However, the feudal monarchs, viziers, samurai, and barons, like the caveman, never imagined, or admitted, that the world could have a different organization or a different way of life and relationships from those they supported and imposed on the world, each to his own world.

"During this time, experimental science, superimposed on the appearances of an immutable power, replaced tradition, philosophy, mysticism, faith, or reflection."

In this context, experimental science has developed mechanics, enabled the great maritime discoveries, created the machine, making it an essential tool of production, and thus imposing a new social organisation:

"The new social organization began with the first industrial revolution: the accumulation of capital, making the urban complexes grow around it, creating markets, bringing out the "new barbarians" (the first had destroyed the Roman Empire and overthrown the Asian empires) - the bourgeoisie, rich, but removed from the privileges of monopolization by the elite of the feudal order. In this context (imperative history or human evolution), the bourgeoisie ended up imposing a new social order, directed by itself, which held capital - capitalism - or by the state, which appropriated it - socialism. The concentration of capital dictated the new civilization - the new forms of life expressed in social organization, in culture, in the arts, in philosophy, in short in all areas of human life."

However, like tribal chiefs, or the masters of ancient empires; like feudal lords, monarchs or tsars, the new masters of the order of capital - socialist or bourgeois - find it hard to realize that the world has changed with the advent of new technologies, which has propelled history towards a new reality, the post-technological world that awaits the advent of a new social organization, new forms of social relations, adapted to the reality provoked by technology itself.

Is the destiny of the elites the blindness imposed by interests and the defense of the status that benefits them, even if this defense leads them to the destruction and rupture of the process, in obvious conflict with evolution - which is an obvious imposition of all nature and human history?

Although the technological revolution that has taken place, with its consequences, constitutes the greatest transformation ever seen in the history of humanity, the beneficiaries of the current social organization, the holders of technology, wealth and power, imitating their predecessors, resist realizing that change is imperative and inevitable. Furthermore, like their predecessors, they imagine that the current form of life, or social organization that benefits them, has stopped history and established itself as a permanent, or final, organization of society.

By repeating the mistakes of the past, they do not imagine, they do not propose and they do not promote the necessary transformation, and this causes the growth of dysrhythmia and the imbalances worsen, which will end up swallowing them up with the systems they represent.

If he persists in not understanding the process, or in resisting change, a deepening of the crisis will be inevitable. The crises, insecurity or threats that afflict the world can only be the beginning of a new process of rupture, whose contours, price and results are unimaginable, because being determined by the dimension of technology, they will be different from anything that has happened in the past.

Therefore, it is necessary that those who act on society or those who lead it in all sectors are convinced of this: the change of civilization, required by the mass of universal consciousness and imposed by the current technological scene, is in the logic of history; its urgency is in the logic of the acceleration of change; its meaning goes in the direction of the anthropological vocation, which evolves from violence and the struggle for survival to higher levels of human fulfillment and conviviality, in accordance with the fundamental principles of universal nature, in search of balance, harmonic awareness, solidarity and participation.

2.2. THE PRESENT TIME

• Competition, concentration, and global threats.

The speed and scale of the technological revolution, which has not been accompanied by the same revolution of civilization in the framework of institutions - and of the human being, has brought, as a consequence, an enormous disturbance in the processes of coexistence.

Thus, the principles of concentration and competition, which ordered social organization and relations during the industrial revolution, product of the steam engine and the accumulated capital - which the machine-generated - continue to order the same social organization and its relations, despite the technological changes that have led us to a new era. Such a distortion, generating disturbances in the process, is aggravated, if we consider the consequences of the dimension, speed and growth of concentration that the new technology has allowed, or has produced, in the hands of those who legitimately or illegitimately dominate it.

In the times of the industrial revolution, the principles of competition and concentration could be, or were even adequate because the power, as well as the speed of competition and concentration that the small size of the technology of the time ensured, were limited. Competition strengthened those who competed, because of certain equality between competitors, and concentration was only relative, because of the limits of the ability to compete, according to the limits of technology. **Nowadays, concentration eliminates competitors and therefore produces a process of unlimited concentration. This is the first difference.**

Without even counting the millennia or centuries that characterized the changes in civilization in the past, the twenty-first century, a little over a century after the advent of the industrial era, has had to deal with the consequences of the new technological revolution. The new technological revolution has transformed the world, or reality, more than the invention of the iron or metals, much more than the advent of empires, Christianity or other factors that overthrew classical antiquity, and immensely more than the invention of the steam engine, the great discoveries, even the scientific renaissance, which prevailed over the feudal era and gave rise to the industrial revolution.

The new chemistry and the new physics have conquered matter and the limits of space; the capacity for continuous innovation compresses time, bringing the past and the future closer together, now concentrated in the present; biology leads to genetic engineering, which allows the control of life by manipulating its mysteries, from conception to death; the technological revolution, in short, has produced a transformation of reality, during these 50 years, greater than ever before in human history, except from a point of view that would span millennia after millennia.

In the midst of this revolution, for the first time in history, man has globalized in space and time. Over time, it has ensured that today's innovation is a simple and immediate consequence of yesterday's causes and that it produces the new realities that will shape tomorrow - transforming change and cause and effect into a continuous and uninterrupted process. In space, man is simultaneously present everywhere on the planet and, increasingly, in the Universe, for the moment, thanks to the instantaneity of communication and the speed of transport: I am referring to omnipresence. The future, today, is still within the limits of fiction.

This immediacy of human presence in time and space makes the human process and its relationships much more complex and at the same time much more interdependent.

These are dimensions that are absolutely compatible with the vocation of man, called to enlarge his space of evolution, towards pluralism and the freedom that derives from it; and they are compatible with the anthropological imperative of evolution from the simple to the complex, ordered by conscience. In this context, already analysed, we can see that the technological revolution is moving in the direction of the evolution of humanity and of all nature.

But we can also check that we are moving in the opposite direction, when technology is used to condition, monopolize, unify or make the process chaotic, rather than harmonious.

This happens because, as in the past, many of those who govern or condition humanity show a certain difficulty in understanding the meaning, scope and implications of change, of which man himself is the author and object. Consequently, because of this difficulty, with regard to the organization of society, the appropriate coexistence with the environment, or the knowledge of oneself and the positioning of each one on oneself, therefore said, in relation to the civilizational order, man continues in the stage preceding the technological changes and behaves, or structures the social organization and its relations, as if the technological changes had not existed.

Consequently, the technology used in favour of the process of concentration, contrary to the direction of the evolution of man and nature (pluralism, diversity, freedom), puts humanity in danger of being subjected to a new form of totalitarianism, or a new form of world dictatorship, much more absolute than anything that has ever existed, and with an aggravating factor: the dictators of the past, without being worldly, had the scepter and the crown, or wore the fateful mustache, which allowed them to be carried to public execution. Now, this is no longer the case. And this we shall see later.

In the post-technological era, the global dictatorship becomes a virtual monopoly and hides behind systems, nameless, faceless and soulless. **The new tyrants dominate the economy, think for everyone, dictate culture, ethics, customs, impose values and imagine, or try to become the world's policemen, in favour of their own interests. They wound pluralism, castrate man's creative capacity, dehumanize the process, generate imbalances and insecurity, which can lead the human process to break down.**

• The results of the process and the virtual economy.

Analysis of the current facts shows the results of this process.

Competition and concentration without limits, therefore, produce the elimination of competitors, generate exclusion, in an increasing process. The numbers of this process show that the speed with which this happens for concentration is much higher than the conditions for the increase in the production of goods and services; and the will of those who possess them, to allow them to be distributed, with a minimum of equity. On the contrary.

The process of concentration, the mechanisms by which it absorbs the goods produced, no matter where they are produced, includes another form of concentration and exclusion: purely virtual goods and wealth are created as a result of the speed of information, which allows or generates speculation. This type of economy produced by the speed of information controls the game of the stock market and adds to the speculative mechanisms that generate exorbitant interest and costs, widening the space of the virtual economy - the new form of inflation borne by the excluded, and further widening the misery in increasing circular order. From this new form of economy - the virtual economy, or speculative, or inflation, which is taking place all over the world, the peripheral regions are excluded, since they do not control the systems, and instead become the instruments of food through the mechanisms imposed on them by the masters and beneficiaries of this new form of the economy; more a game and speculation than economy.

According to the conviction of some people, for the defense of the virtual economy, the information would be a good and a product like any other, therefore an economic good. But information, gambling or speculation do not feed a third of the world who suffer from hunger, or do not give shelter, health and well-being to those who live, only at the level of survival, those who now total several billion human beings. There is a lack of concepts, forms and instruments capable of transforming virtual goods into economic, or social goods, which could otherwise be accessed by the poor, at least significant parts of the company, making the factors purely speculative.

As long as this does not change, the virtual economy will not go beyond mere speculation, generating a global financial round whose price, or a new form of inflation, is paid by the excluded, sucked into the accumulation process and subjected to its rules. These rules support policies to guarantee virtual (speculative) systems, but ignore or make it difficult for the excluded to be included and participate. A good example of these cruel and harmful rules is the requirement of the dominant systems, imposed on the debtors, to generate untouchable primary surpluses at the price of increasing exclusion, poverty and inhuman living conditions of billions of people, in addition to the 100 or so peripheral countries, transformed into new slaves or mere colonies of the technological age, which help to finance the systems.

All this is accepted as ethical and sustainable.

This explains, better than any eloquence, the almost geometric growth of the debt of the excluded world, a debt whose costs are the main channel through which poor and dependent countries are drained into virtual economies, imposed by the rich, those who dominate the financial systems - or technology, create or manipulate information, establish criteria, generate risks and results, according to their interests. This point of view also better explains, on the one hand, the growing misery and exclusion that affects the world, generating the imbalances that threaten the survival of the process, and on the other hand, the worsening crises that threaten to bring the process to a halt.

This drainage, to cite one case - the Brazilian one, already exceeds, by far, the 100 billion reals per year - an important part of the GDP, and an amount well above 50% of the total public investment available to make its own development possible. This figure, in addition to the debt of the peripheral world, exceeds one thousand billion dollars. It is for issues of such a nature and magnitude that fashionable economic and social theories present justifications, but do not present solutions or alternatives. And this is so because they are based on competition, concentration and the purely financial, or market, vision that has become the goal of society as a whole, or of any human relationship. For this reason, we don't see the future - where the process is going and what the outcome will be. They prefer to act or act as if the future does not exist. Their point of view on the process reaches, at most, today or tomorrow, but not the future.

This happens because at the base or root of the system, in addition to the interests of its beneficiaries, there are obsolete theories, fixed in the concepts that preceded the technological revolution, which do not realize that the system is based on the interests of its beneficiaries or perceive, but do not consider - its consequences, and whose dynamics contrast with the immobility of necessary conceptual changes, as a prerequisite for the production of concrete and operational changes. Some representative figures of the concentration and the process of exclusion due to this dynamic, will show the tragic consequences of this system which, for many reasons, is maintained and applied in the post-technological world, although its origins and foundations go back to the time of the railway trains, the stagecoaches or the good guy who, revolver in hand, faced the representatives of evil.

That's true - and the hint is aware of it.

American President George W. Bush, the most representative of the resistance to this civilization and the multiple global operating systems, by dividing the world into the forces of good and evil, threatens to bring the world back to the dawn of the Middle Ages - to the adolescence of history, bringing back the inquisition and the fire to that tragic Manichaeism by which the system sees, interprets and intends to build history.

• The initial concentration and exclusion numbers.

The numbers of concentration and exclusion, and thus of the imbalance that threatens global sustainability or security, are evident in any statistics that show what is happening in the world. The following figures are taken from the **United Nations Human Development Report** and show the speed at which the process of concentration is taking place. The UN report is from 1998, and the commentary is from "**The Third World Revolution**".

Millennium", which I am transcribing. Some numbers may have changed since then, but not in a dimension that would demonstrate any change in the process. Moreover, in analyzing the process, in a broader series, **The Third Millennium Revolution** refers to the 1980 UNESCO report cited in "**The Age of Man**".

This report shows that concentration and exclusion is a seemingly irreversible process, which is worsening and shows no indication that "the cake would grow', or that 'the economy would stabilise' - expressions so fashionable among concentration mentors - that it would be distributed later, in a second phase - always in a second phase - in the next half-year, next year, next decade...

I'm transcribing bits and pieces from "**The Age of Man**".

Bill Gates, the owner of Microsoft, is among the 200 richest people in the world, accumulating $500,000 per second, now with assets in excess of $1 trillion, worth a thousand times the average annual income of many countries - not the poorest.

The 200 richest people in the world, who in 1994 accumulated 400,000 million dollars, and who today, accumulate an income of about 1.042 billion dollars, concentrate a third more than the Brazilian GDP, or an amount equivalent to the additional income of a third of the population of the Planet, or 2 billion people.

Moreover, a recent study on the distribution of wealth in Brazil, organized by several Universities, including USP and Unicamp, stated that 1.2 million Brazilian families hold 40% of the national GDP. As we can see, the problem is also that of national economies, not only that of the world economy.

Further on:

As for the poorest 20% of the world's population, which thirty years ago had 2.3% of the world's income, their share has now been reduced to just 1.4%. On the other hand, over the same period, the share of the richest 20% of the world's wealth increased from 62% to 82%.

These figures are quite worrying - perhaps they should be terrifying, and they are heading towards rupture, if this perverse process of concentration/exclusion is not reversed.

Let's look at other features of the same process[13]:

It is not only wealth that is concentrated and whose concentration leads to exclusion. The speed at which concentration is increasing is higher than the rate of growth of wealth - some estimates say that concentration is increasing somewhere around 5% per year, while the growth of world wealth is less than 3%, and this makes the process more serious: wealth is growing more in rich countries than in poor countries, absorbing some of the small growth in these countries. The same is true with regard to knowledge and technology. In 1998, 95% of patents were in the hands of the industrialised countries, leaving 5% for the rest of the world.

It is therefore not possible, in this system, to maintain the rules of competition in the face of concentrated technology, whose potential benefits always arrive too late and at unbearable costs; or simply in the face of technology that never reaches the weakest competitors - the increasingly excluded.

The process of concentration occurs in all sectors and in all directions: the process of mergers and acquisitions of companies is another channel through which wealth and power continue to be concentrated.

---

[13] At the closing of the revision of this book, it was announced, in Japan, the merger of UFJ Holdings Inc. with Bank of Tokyo - Mitsubishi, whose assets amount to $1.7 trillion, a value equivalent to twice the Brazilian GDP - all that is produced in terms of wealth in Brazil. That is more than Brazil, but exclusively financial. There are no people, no territory, no natural wealth. But there is power. Only power.

The analyses of "**The Third Millennium Revolution**", based on the table presented in this edition, already four years ago, warned about the fact that

the merger of some banks would add assets concentrated around $240 billion. In 1999, the merger of Bank of America and the Bank of Nations alone generated assets of $524 billion.

The following year, the announced merger of the associated Japanese banks generated assets of $1.3 trillion, and the European stock markets, if it were to occur, as announced - and which is likely to happen one day - would have to manage assets of around $7 trillion. Now, 7 trillion dollars is an amount nine times higher than Brazil's GDP and more than one time the GDP of the United States, that is to say, about one fifth (1/5) of the world's wealth. In whose hands? How much of the real economy and the virtual economy?*

This process, if it is not reversed, will continue to occur more and more severely, because it will continue to occur faster and faster, until it is broken, for its own unsustainability, as a result of the imbalance generated. And any imbalance, in all nature, as mentioned above, has a natural tendency to break, if it is not corrected in time.

The book points out the small scandal of the occasional 240 billion in assets accumulated by the merger process and the fact that the mergers announced at the time would accumulate more than thirty times that amount without scandalizing anyone or anything at that point. These facts simply turned into routine news or current events, or from analysts initiated into the market, communicators or media commentators, happy in their delirium with the figures and their dimension, without realizing the process and its consequences on this civilization. It is a question here of the fact that all that remains to be seen are appearances, conjunctures, because "thinking hurts" (return to perception, almost a prophecy by Fernando Pessoa).

The most serious thing is that this one, the concentrated economy, is for the most part "rotten", to use a common term. It is a simple accounting exercise, which is reinforced by the virtual economy, which grows or is generated according to the speed of information, or the role-playing that generates speculation, information and play that, moreover, it is increasingly difficult to identify to whom they belong, who controls them, how they are administered, and in favour of what. Of course, much of it has to be, for example, by the war industry, by the maintenance of power, thanks to the growing concentration, which allows it to be the police of the world, or to take the place of human values, or the meaning of life, in a process that is absurd because it lacks reason or purpose.

Where are we going?

I know some people aren't looking for answers. The sight of their horizons does not go beyond the blinkers that limit their perspectives. This is not, however, the perspective of the human species.

In any case, there will be those who argue that the virtual economy is a possible theory or reality.

The question is - in this virtual reality, or theory, whether the existing human structures and relationships are appropriate for virtual reality, whether it has already generated a theory appropriate for virtual reality and whether the processes can be sufficient, or whether they can survive virtualization without this new theory.

Meanwhile, human structures, relationships and needs are concrete and have balance, pluralism and freedom as their essential vocation, which contrasts with monotheism the uniformity of global systems, according to the interests that concentration imposes.

I return to some analyses of the "**Third Millennium Revolution**", which follow:

Thirty years ago UNESCO[14] was also scandalized by the fact that the average income of the rich countries was more than 100 times higher than that of the poor countries.
The average income of the poorest countries ($9,000 in the USA versus $70 in Tanzania). Today, this difference is more than 300 times higher (25,000 dollars in the USA, against the same 70 dollars in Tanzania). However, this is taken for granted by the media and their global commentators, delighted by the power of concentration and the awareness, or lack thereof, of leaders and those who run the systems. For them, this is only a marginal issue - one that deserves no more comment than a brief, always less important than the swings of the New York Stock Exchange or any other stock exchange or the

---

[14] UNESCO- General Conference, 21st Meeting, Belgrade, 1980. Preliminary report by the Director-General on the Medium-Term Plan for 1984-1989 - in "The Age of Man".

reliability index established, circumstantially, by instruments serving the same systems and their interests.

*Meanwhile - **the Third Millennium Revolution** continues - the process of suppression increases proportionally. UN figures show that more than 2 billion people in the world today live below the level of poverty, **going beyond the injustice of such an inhuman condition** - the expression is from the United Nations Human Development Report, 1998, condemned to live on less than 2 dollars a day to satisfy all their needs - or at least the basic rights of survival and a minimum of dignity or human dimension.*

In proportion to the concentration of wealth, the number of those living in this condition, however, grows rapidly, as analyzed below:

If the process of concentration-exclusion is not reversed, over the next 50 years, more than 4 billion people will be added to the 2 billion excluded today because they will be born in Africa, Asia, Latin America, not in the United States or Northern Europe.

It is better to alert, in this perspective, so that the new Centers of Power - the new world of business towers - can be prepared, because this legion of outcasts will come. These figures are not fiction. They will happen in this generation and in the next if the Centers of Power remain insensitive or incompetent, or without an effective will to reverse the process. Or they will not happen, because before then the rupture will come. Or perhaps the era of solidarity, participation, cooperation and deconcentration may come if these concepts prevail, in spite of themselves - centers or masters of power, who are not aware of them, or only as strong expressions but without a meaning capable of inspiring the changes necessary for the viability of the process.

At the very least, the intellectuals and analysts of society and its processes, not only of the market, would have to address these questions in order to formulate alternative paths or solutions, working from and integrated into the global consciousness.

And the text continues, now referring to the case of Brazil, to show that the issue of exclusion and unequal distribution of income, in addition to being a global problem, occurs in the internal structure of countries. See the dimension of the Brazilian case.

In this context, and in Brazil, which is being built in the footsteps of concentration, it is not a figure of speech to say that Brazil is the world champion country of concentration and, consequently, of the poor distribution of income.

*This fact is proved by the table on page 130 of the **Third Millennium Revolution** and transcribed on page 85 of this book, which shows that "the ratio of the average share of the richest 10% and the poorest 40%, which in Japan, or Belgium is 1:3 or 1:4 in Bangladesh, or 1:21 in Costa Rica, or 1:28 in Kenya, is in Brazil 1:30.*

In reality, in the process by which Brazil is led or pushed, like so many other peripheral countries, a caudal country of the global systems, especially of the virtual or speculative economy, the theory is practiced that it is necessary to strengthen competitiveness in order to conquer markets, or balance sheets equilibrium. Therefore, it is necessary to concentrate, even if in order to concentrate we must exclude, or proclaim the elimination of exclusion as an objective to be achieved and thus bring hope to the excluded.

We do not realize that this is the logic of global interests, replacing human interests or rights. It is the logic of the terrible misconception that only profit - finance, constitutes the meaning of life of men and society and is capable of moving them. By this mistaken logic, millions of human beings are allowed to die, or are killed by malnutrition - hunger and the diseases it produces; by this logic, the wars and suffering of the world are provoked into a truly global genocide; 40,000 people, especially children, die every day, just for these reasons. This fact means that, in 150 days, 7 million people are killed by the system that makes them die, as many as Hitler sent to the crematoriums in 4 or 5 years. Not that the genocide committed by Hitler is a minor crime in the genocide for which he answers to history. But it is that an equivalent crime, no matter how much bigger or smaller - but more diffuse - it continues to be committed, without the same global repulsion.

This generation, our generation, will have to answer to civilization for having allowed the system that commits genocide on such a scale to continue indefinitely, without even sufficiently challenging it. We must ask ourselves why there is so much irrationality in the consciousness of men, attached to old theories, either escaping from reality that a minimum of analysis or critical posture makes evident, or obstinately persisting in worn-out errors such as the one that says that we must let "the cake swell", to then distribute it, a very effective formula for maintaining the system of interests, and its unsustainable results.

The book goes on to cite other examples, now taken from daily life or the news, which coldly record the process of increasing concentration and the economics of speculation, as if they were normal and necessary systems. The book refers, in this case, to the banking system - the mechanism that best expresses the notion of profit that drives financial systems and on which policies are based, which, obediently, submit to it. The analysis says:

In November 2001, the IE[15] newspaper published an interesting table showing that the Brazilian citizen, who for eight years had invested 100 reals in the main support of Brazilian social programs - the savings account, would today have 324 reals in the same account. However, if over the same period of time he owed the same 100 reals to the banking system, by being overdrawn, for example, he would owe the system 160,000 reals. That's right - he would have 324.00 reals in profit for him, but he would have 160,000 reals in debt against him.

For this and similar reasons, a study published in the same context by another magazine, Época[16], shows that the invoicing of Brazilian banks in the first half of 2001 increased by 10.2%, while the revenues of the production sector increased by only 1%. In the same period, the net profit of the financial system increased by 18.3%, while the profit of the productive sector fell by 33.9%.

In the same year, it was observed that the ERP mechanism, which supports the banking system, transferred to the banks about R$20 billion, of which the adjusted and corrected amount should be around R$35 billion. This does not make much of a difference, contrary to the argument, if these resources were not taken from the Treasury or the Central Bank reserves, but from the pockets of taxpayers or businesses. In any case, they were taken out of the

---

[15] Editora Abril - Isto é - Novembro de 2001
[16] Editora Globo

Brazilian economy and therefore out of society, concentrating ... concentrating and excluding ...[17]

All this is justified as a theory, a science of economics, or a way to balance the economic "equation".

We can, again, ask ourselves: What kind of economy is this one? What science of economics or social organization? What rationality makes it possible to tackle the process, and to imagine being able then to remedy its consequences, or to suddenly produce the miracle of converting the systems of concentration and humanizing them?

At the same time, the poverty eradication program has had difficulty in allocating R$ 4 billion, much of it under the guise of investment in health infrastructure and other regular programs.

To save the pension system, the pension contribution is established unilaterally modifying a perfect contract and just because the economy, speculation is untouchable - the primary surplus ...

Today, in Brazil, and with some global repercussions, the Zero Hunger program has been introduced - as if hunger was the cause and not the consequence of this system.

Meanwhile, the legion of those who are excluded by the system maintained, the system of concentration, of the free market, or of financial speculation, is growing, thus increasing the number of applicants in the queues for hunger, land, housing, citizenship, human dignity, blatant proof of the system's inability to provide men with employment and income - the prerequisites of equal dignity, freedom, or, in the final analysis, democracy - the regime of equality, or dignity - replaced by numbers of alms given and marketed and for the maintenance of hope that change will come tomorrow.

---

[17] The concentration system continues. The profits of the financial system reached something close to 20 billion Reais in 2003, and those of Petrobras - the Brazilian multinational that is governed, not by national reality, but by international oil speculation, exceeded 17 billion dollars. The benefits of the system credit card charges increased by 17%. While Brazil's GDP grew by less than 1% and employee income declined.

Finally, from this point of view of essential policies summarized from the financial system, and human relations reduced to profit, or to the market, Brazil - to continue with the same example, spends 10% of its annual GDP to pay debt interest rates, nearly 5% guaranteed by primary surplus priority over all things, including human dignity, while, in order to feed the system, it maintains interest rates at levels which, in the Middle Ages, would lead many to be burned at the stake for the crime of usury, or to hell for the same sin. Today, analysts, communicators and marketing systems, as well as leader's subject to the market, call this distortion monetary policy, and alms and welfare, they call it social policy. I cite one last, very recent and very specific example to show how the marketing systems maintained by the systems conceal reality from society.

In reality, the resources of society are being ripped out of it, by all means, in an attempt to plug the holes of speculation, while the resources for the speculative economy - the primary surplus without any reparation - are counted in hundreds of billions of reals, and even spoken of with a certain pride of "duty done", as if it were possible to confuse the nation or the State with the class of primary school pupils.

I will give the last example: an official marketing medium was circulating at the time of the debate on the contribution to social security for pensioners, which proclaimed, also grandiloquently, that R$ 60 billion would be provided by this measure - which would definitively resolve the issue of this official body. To silence the protests of the most attentive, the support added in small print or in a weak voice, the half-truth, "in the next 20 years". One could also call this, in addition to "market ethics", "marketing ethics" which, as we can see, follows market ethics: both do not exist - because for marketing propagators, as for market propagators, this notion makes no sense. However, according to data published by the Social Security at the same time, the debt of large companies, which did not declare their income or pay their taxes, was close to R$ 200 billion. Against them, the applauded and life-saving reform did nothing, concentrated as it was on extorting people rather than demanding systems.

The examples cited are a good sample of how the system helps to consolidate the virtual economy and its speculative arms which, globalised, dominate, or claim to dominate the world, even at the expense of the excluded, devoured by the whirlwind of concentration, or speculation of all kinds, the virtual, that of the market or of ignorance, stemming from one's own exclusion.

This reference to Brazil becomes important because, given the size of its resources and for other reasons, Brazil, in collaboration with countries in similar circumstances and capacities, could play an important role in reversing this process that is moving towards rupture and it could make a significant contribution, Brazil, towards the change of civilization, the alternative for survival and for the humanization of society. This if it understood its potential role.

3. IMMOBILITY OF SOCIAL THEORIES AND SIGNS OF RUPTURE.

The unsustainability of the current model

I am now transcribing the very current analysis also presented in "**The Revolution of the Third Millennium**", which updated the analyses already made and proposed 20 years ago in "**The Age of Man**".

The numbers of the process, and their trend, show that maintaining the principle of the freedom to concentrate according to the competitive power of each, is an unsustainable principle in the post-technological era, just as the principle of competition is unsustainable, therefore, supporting concentration, especially because, if the current trend and pace of concentration and exclusion of competitors continues, soon there will be no more competitors. This means that, in the post-technological era, the principle of competition has become an autophagic principle, which is destroying itself, because instead of strengthening and multiplying competitors, it is eliminating them until, if possible, there are none left.

In reality, just as the principles of concentration and competition, strategies of domination, or control of the world, are also unsustainable. They fall into a historical error, the beneficiaries of the current system, thinking that the policies put in place by US President George W. Bush are the best expression, an obvious instrument of the central systems of power. In reality, the "condottiere" of the largest beneficiary country of the systems, by promoting the strategy of war, or human relations based on force, threat or the power of arms, do not realize that, each with the weapons at their disposal, the masters of the systems and the excluded, or the masters of the system and those who act outside it. The masters of systems promote war; those who fight them use the diffuse weapons capable of spreading terror - just the form of warfare that is within their reach, leading it to the heart, or to the centers of power, threatening them as much as the centers of power threaten them. What does it matter if thousands of people die in the explosion of the New York towers, or the bombs dropped as a global spectacle in front of the media on the people of Iraq, Iran, Vietnam, or the Balkans, for the reasons or ambushes of war which, in its essence, is nothing more than institutionalized terrorism?

What a world of freedom this is - where the security of any head of state is comparable to a war operation - the people contained by barricades or obstacles of all kinds, while the gathering of the powerful - The G7, for example, can only take place with similar operations, wherever they take place; or, finally, what freedom is that, where people live in bunkers, with fear and anxiety about what may come tomorrow or even tonight?

The "**Third Millennium Revolution**" already analysed it:

When a blade in someone's pocket is able to reach the heart of power; when a blister, developed in any laboratory, is able to decimate humanity, more than the Black Death in the Middle Ages ; or when information hacked into a global network, or a button pressed, or a cloned code, is capable of building or destroying Nations, economies, or any form of coexistence, think or act as we thought and acted in the pre-technological age, this is probably a negation of the evolutionary capacity of the human species, if this process was sustainable and imposed on future generations. It would mean increasing the gap that unbalances the planet, or precipitating the breakdown of the process on a global scale, through the power of technology and its inevitable consequence: globalization and the interdependence of all things.

Thereafter:

"However, this is what happens, apart from the official reasons, their analyses, interpretations and justifications. The concepts of those who dominate, or imagine dominating the world, are a repetition of the concepts known and practiced in the nineteenth century or in previous centuries, when they were generated in the pre-technological era, or in the age of the distant first industrial revolution - the tanks and trains in the Wild West, based on the conquest of the West, or of large cities, or in the colonialism of "the sun that does not set on His Majesty's empire"; from the time when servitude or slavery was accepted and practiced, when awareness of human rights was, at most, a moral imperative and the equality of peoples and nations, or their rights, did not exist and concepts of justice were only valid for the elites and still depended on their ability to impose themselves, through court or other maneuvers.

It must be understood that technology had to come to liberate humanity from these concepts, not to condition it more and more to them. We could talk about liberation technology, or for liberation, as an alternative. Why not, Leonardo Boff?

The routine of repeating the past.

The current mentors of the systems, the so-called dictators, through the mechanisms they dominate and the wealth and power they concentrate, continue, however, to imagine that they can maintain their control over the rest of the world. I give some striking examples of this way of thinking, starting a little before the Bush era, a short-lived mistake of the American nation, for which I reserve a few comments at the end - as an extreme expression of a new colonialism, which imagines bringing to our days this concept of "empire where the sun does not set". Trying to achieve this goal, the owners of the systems use technology and its power to focus, as a form of domination, while as a threat, on those who do not conform, or submit to their global interests. What they do not know is that the post-technological era is not a new era of domination already more compatible with global control, which only generates insecurity and revolt in the world. In reality, the effectiveness of these controls will only be maintained in the exact proportion in which they eliminate freedom, in favour of a new fundamentalism that takes on the face of defending that same freedom or democracy, and which in reality they wound to death.

I am now looking at the new ideology of power, starting, as I said, just before the Bush era, and quoting again from **The Third Millennium Revolution**.

*In 1999, President Bill Clinton in Florence at the meeting of the so-called Third Way presidents said, **"Let the poor not delude themselves - investments will go where they bring the greatest profits."** He wasn't even original in his statement, or his threat, it's not clear.*

*Keneth Galbraith at UnB in 1976 said, **"It is better to be exploited by Volkswagen than to be exploited by no one. Rather than not having multinationals, it is better to have them, even if they exploit us. "***

That too was not original. In the 1920's, Calvin Coolidge, President of the United States - we see that this is a line of thinking that dominates the process

*- was adamant: **"Everybody needs to know this: America's business is to do business."***

He was not saying anything new. Adam Smith, originally in England in 1846, in "the empire where the sun never sets", advised the English nobles, "to the children of the old families, who had accumulated wealth, agreed with the policy of colonialism, because in the colonies they could invest their wealth and reap the benefits".

Don't let the poor fool themselves... and, see, all this was before the Bush era[18].

But let's continue with the "Third Millennium Revolution":

150 years ago, in 1854, Native leader Seattle wrote to U.S. President Franklin Pierce - the latter proposed to him to buy his land: "How is it that one can buy or sell the sky, the heat of the earth! This idea seems strange to us..." and he continued: "When the Great Chief in Washington sends to tell us that he wants to buy our land, he asks too much of us".

Among many other examples of strength and dignity, we cannot cite that of the Turkish Government recently in President Bush's strategy to invade Iraq.

To obtain military bases in Turkey, the US President has offered to pay $26 billion. According to news agencies, the Turkish government demanded $32 billion.

The value of "national consciousness" would be that? Or would it be auctioned off for that value? Or the business theory of property... I don't think it is the value of the parcel of the mass consciousness of the Turkish people. Nor do I

---

[18]From the book "Tous aux abris !", by Michael Moore - Palme d'Or at the Cannes Film Festival - I collect, at the last moment, this concept by Dick Cheney, Vice-President and Mr Bush's foreign policy guru:
"About 70 to 75 percent of our business is energy-related, serving customers such as Unocal, Exxon, Shell, Chevron and many others among the world's leading oil companies.
"As a result, we often have to operate in very difficult places. Our Lord has not seen fit to put oil and gas only in places where there are democratically elected governments friendly to the United States. Sometimes we have to work in places where, considering all the obstacles, no one would like to work. But we go where the business is" (Ceto Institute conference, June 23, 1998.)

believe that the "national conscience" has made Jose Maria Aznar of Spain or the new Chamberlain of England - Tony Blair, or the little Duce of Italy - Berlusconi act to extend the red carpet to the passage of the war tanks in Iraq, another war based on lies and the deception, under the guise of human rights or democracy. We'll go where the business is...

To each one, history or the mass of consciousness, will make one's postures pay. However, continues **The Third Millennium Revolution**:

But what to expect from the man who, in 2000, then candidate for Grand Chief in Washington, the same George W. Bush, in the debate on television, proposed the exchange of the debt of poor third world countries for a part of their natural resources (or sod their land?) repeating exactly the proposal of his ancestor Franklin Pierce, 145 years ago?

George W. Bush must not have read the letter from Seattle. Or, if he did, he didn't understand it. Or he simply understood and turned a deaf ear, inspired by a story that made violence and conquest a constant, and land trade - a trade above all, the complement of what the armed force had failed to conquer.

It is worth remembering that the formation of American territory - half of it, was the result of wars of conquest, or trade, the purchase or exchange of territories or interests. As can be seen, the alliance of the interests of war and finance is not a new strategy. As a result of this alliance, the United States, are the territories of New York, Louisiana and western Mississippi, Alaska, Florida, Texas, New Mexico, California, Nevada, Utah, Arizona and part of the states of Oregon and Wyoming. Nor can we ignore the fact that during the era of colonialism, the First World War allowed the United States to extend its domination over ephemeral colonies: the Philippines, Guam, Samoa and Hawaii - a small empire in the Pacific and also Puerto Rico in the Caribbean. It did not have time to develop and consolidate its old-style colonial empire, as this trend had already been exhausted. But he left a legacy and heirs.

Colonialism has taken other forms in the post-technological era; more sophisticated means, such as technology, and other means much larger than technology, such as finance, or the speculation, or global systems - the Bretton Woods agreements, the monopoly of nuclear technology, and other weapons of destruction; the use of diplomatic pressure, exerted on the weakest. But even so, the new forms of colonialism do not dispense with the tragic legacy of explicit forms of armed interventionism, if this maintains or extends power, as we have seen in Iraq, and as we have seen in Iran, Afghanistan, or in the frustrated attempts of Vietnam, Korea or Cuba, always in the name of freedom, democracy, or Christian civilization, prostituted and turned into an effective instrument to maintain the alliance of arms and commercial interests. **Let the poor not deceive themselves!**

There is no xenophobia or anti-Americanism in this analysis. It is simply the memory of facts that allow us to better understand the process, because history repeats itself, instead of moving forward. In this process, however, the United States is, at this crucial moment, the main actor and, without knowing it, we cannot understand the plot. So we cannot fail to analyse them.

Some historians admit that history repeats, indeed, but they warn that the repetition of history often takes the form of a farce and, what is more serious, often, too, by repeating itself, it turns into tragedy.

In the context of the repetition of the past and the ignorance and denial of the dimensions of the post-technological era or the threats that hang over the present and grow to the future, it is better understood that the rejection of the Kyoto Protocol has a long and well-founded origin, so that the separation of men between the representatives of evil and good (the bandits and the good guys); the resurrection of Cold War or armed security concepts or strategies in the context of the economic massacre of countries such as Argentina, as Mexico was before, the weakest part of NAFTA, an example of what Latin America could become in the FTAA, as a system of domination rather than cooperation, while the arm of the IMF imposes its recessive and exclusionary policies on the poor, the virtual economy dictates its interest rates, generating unsustainable debts, and the Bretton Woods Agreement continues to impose its world monetary organization, as long as it is supported by the booming economy of the smaller allies - (Vae Victis), and the excluded, who have to support the global inflation of speculative money.

All this under the threat of the monopoly of the bomb and weapons of mass destruction. Disarmed the weakest, which seems and is, essentially, good - who is going to disarm the Lord of the Empire, and his faithful squires?

These concepts and facts show that in this post-technological era, or the global dimension of systems, the principles of concentration and competition cannot be maintained, going against the nature of the human process and all its circumstances in the name of free market, liberalism, state socialism and all the "neo" forms they generate, giving everything and all the power to one without admitting sharing, equality, pluralism and freedom.

Globalization, terror and signs of rupture.

It is not globalization that is unsustainable. Unsustainable are the principles, overtaken by the technological revolution, that continue to be applied in the era of globalization, and the bad strategies practiced to keep them. We must give globalisation its true meaning.

The true meaning of globalization, made possible by the technological revolution, should produce the **universal** inclusion of people in the process of human and social evolution, of the diversity and plurality of their relationships, behaviours, economies and cultures. It should mean an overall increase in relations between persons and between peoples, in a society that is complex because it is evolved, but ordered, because of complementary and harmonic parts, and therefore a truly pluralistic and free society.

- Globalization, therefore, should mean the growth of pluralism, participation, cooperation and freedom and not the strengthening of exclusive, monopolistic and totalitarian concentration.

The post-technological world cannot sustain its globalism through the threat of nuclear warheads, or the manipulation of genes, monopolized by one. This hypothesis requires the adoption of new structures and a new ethic, inspired by law, institutions, organization and human relations, on a personal, national and international level. This new ethic and this new organization will have to allow access for all, which will certainly only be achieved by adopting the principles of solidarity and participation as the only means of ensuring freedom in a pluralist world, shared by all, the diversity of their laws, cultures and identities.

Unity does not mean unanimity. Unity means ordered multiplicity, capable of coexisting in harmony, cooperation and peace. Reaching this stage - it must be repeated so that no doubt remains - means making a revolution in the concepts and practices of the organization and functioning of society, both at the global and local levels, of all peoples, all countries, or of each individual. **This is not a romantic question. Nor is it simply an ethical one. This is an imposition of technology, to ensure survival.**

If such a revolution is underway, through technology, through things, since it cannot be made by men, their organization or their way of coexisting? Why should man be man the false note of nature, including things created by himself? These are necessary questions that cannot be silenced, and before which we cannot remain silent.

It is the lack of understanding of this necessary revolution in concepts and practice, or the lack of courage or the will to make it, that allows, even with the applause of some, that the systems of concentration, desiring to impose themselves on the world, reduce the security, freedom or future of the human species to the spectacle of chasing a man and his Organization from cave to cave, amidst the poverty or misery of the world ; who, in the name of this strategy, share megatons of bombs, put on show by the world media, and bags of bread and medicine, marketed, to cheat hunger and heal the wounds caused by those same bombs; or appeal to the world to rebuild what those same bombs have destroyed. Even if we rebuild things, the people who died or were killed will not rebuild themselves.

It is a tragedy, not a farce, we repeat once again the history of previous hunts, prior to Fidel Castro or Ho Chi Min, or, in the first instance, to the Indians of the West, under the pretext of imposing on the world and on history, power, their own culture, their own conception of good and evil, or the erroneous concept of freedom, which means the submission of the weakest and the unlimited power of the strongest, all in favour of profit, in favour of business...

It is against this repetition of the past, in relation to the dimension and power of technology, **that the mass of consciousness is formed and turned towards the world.** It is also against pre-potency that, despite other reasons, whether apparent or not, an environment is being created that is conducive to the emergence and action of fundamentalist terrorism, a form that is diverted or desperate for the mass of consciousness.

In this context, it is also better understood that September 11, 2001, a major tragedy only as a warning to mankind, that the world of absolute control belongs to the past and its limited technology, and that only a profound change in the concepts that define history, human beings and their circumstances, can avoid rupture. Of this rupture, September 11 may have been only a beginning, a small sign, given the size of the bill that can be presented and claimed by history, otherwise the process was not reversed.

Sadly, the September 11th attacks produced more than 2,500 fatal casualties in New York City. On that same day, for those who circulated around and had eyes to see beyond the television screens that showed the collapse of the former towers, were on display in the kiosks of the airport of São Paulo, a newspaper of the previous day, displaying the headline: **40,000 children die every day of malnutrition in the world.** Few people - perhaps no one - paid any attention to this headline, or were outraged by the tragedy it announced, because the tragedy of the New York towers was more compressed, reaching into the heart of power, hitting the masters of the systems. It was more spectacular.

The death of children in the world, had no face. Diffuse, death took place in Africa, Southeast Asia, Latin America. Some children would also die in the ghettos of New York, or in London, it is true, but this too did not matter much. It didn't happen to Manhattan, in the heart of New York City, or in the jugular of the system. Therefore, they did not move - or provoke - the perception, horror or solidarity of men. They were not a spectacle for the media. But the tragedy did exist, and every second, death was performing its function on innocent people - as innocent as the victims of the New York Towers, fueled this other tragedy by the greed of men, or by their primal instincts, which maintain the systems that concentrate and exclude, concentrate and concentrate and exclude... until imbalances produce rupture, if the process is not reversed.

PART II

THE PATH OF RUPTURE

1. GROWTH OF THE GAP BETWEEN THOSE WHO CONCENTRATE AND THOSE WHO ARE EXCLUDED

1.1 A REFORMULATION OF THE CONCEPT OF DEVELOPMENT

The process of human development, and therefore the social process in all its dimensions - ethical, political, economic, cultural and all the others that make it up - cannot be considered as a simple economic process, or its interpretation, which, for its part, cannot be summed up in simple indicators of financial stability or of the state of the economy. However, this is what has been done since the concept of the prevalence or dominance of capital, the market, or profit as the supreme value, raison d'être and motive for human actions was introduced, since man has been forgotten in all its dimensions.

This reductionism tries to survive despite the transformations and the stage reached by technology, which should have happened to man and his institutions.

On another level, interpretations and denunciations of a purely ethical nature or intended to awaken consciences to the situations of injustice and imbalance generated by these situations have prevailed. These denunciations and awakening of consciences are important elements for change, because they strengthen the mass of consciousness, but the mass of consciousness itself must know minimally where its aspirations wish or can lead the process, and the paths to get there.

More than twenty years ago, the book **"The Age of Man"** proposed that, among the concepts to be overcome, the concept of development, then in vogue, should be questioned.

That book said:

"We cannot accept a concept of development that ends up being confused with unlimited growth for some, to the detriment of the majority, as if it were necessary and development was limited to that. Or simply a process of

increasing numbers and quantities, leaving man aside, as if he didn't count and it made sense. "

Having more or be more.

The proposal was not new or totally unique. Pope Paul VI, in his encyclical Populorum Progressio[19] more than 10 years ago, warned of the need to replace the concept of development understood as having more with a new concept that encompasses **being more**.

The book "**The Third Millennium Revolution**" comments:

This new concept, however, for a long time was seen only as a moral imperative, and only in the 1980s did it receive significant recognition in the academic and political sectors and, slowly, in economic analyses, which adopted the concept of development only as the product of economic-financial indicators. On this occasion, the United Nations finally began to put the new concept into practice in its analyses and reports - measuring the level of development of the Human Development Index - HDI. The new measurement criteria for this analysis, sought to adopt capable of revealing the real conditions of people's lives and not just economic growth.

Although this concept is now accepted or at least considered theoretically, not even by financial institutions, in practice it is necessary to give this conquest of concepts concrete consequences, namely, in addition to the formation of a new consciousness, to move towards the creation of a new theory of development, which takes into account the human dimensions as the ethical and practical object of this process.

It is necessary to create coherent instruments based on concepts.

However, it is not enough to grasp these new concepts. At the same time, it is necessary to create mechanisms, or specific tools, capable of ensuring that human development, and not simply economic growth, by being made possible, is expressed in the increase in the effective participation of individuals and society in the development process and its benefits.

---

[19]Paul VI - Pope - Encíclica Populorum Progressio - 1967

According to this view, human development is not just a by-product, or an activity, complementary - compensatory or supportive of economic activity. Human development is the object itself and the instrument, or the principal means, of the main social organization and functioning of social relations. The economy must adapt to it, be part of this environment, and we need to develop mechanisms and instruments compatible with this conception. Otherwise, it does not become a concept, a vague desire or a theory.

Developing these instruments or mechanisms is possible.

1.3 UN DENUNCIATIONS.

It is worth reinforcing, at this stage, some of the analyses already presented in the first part of this book, by transcribing, again, some pieces of "The Revolution of the Third Millennium".

The 1996 UN Human Development Report already warned: If current trends continue, the economic differences between industrialized and developing countries will change from unjust to inhuman. Probably in the absence of greater denunciation, the 1998 report refers to the world situation as "grotesque". Personally, I prefer to say tragic, despite the essential identity between extreme tragedy and extreme comedy, between the sublime and the comic, or the grotesque in theatrical language.

The awareness of this fact and the denunciations are old.

As early as 1980, UNESCO - also a UN body - warned us that: "This fact is confirmed when we consider the inequalities between human beings, be they individuals, groups or countries. »

"Economic disparities have not diminished," the UN text said at the time: "In many countries, GDP per capita is less than $300, while in others it is $9,000, or thirty times more. »

Today, in 2000, in some rich countries, the income is not 30, but 100 times higher than the average income of poor countries. Or more than 300 times, as is the case when the average income of countries like the United States or Japan is compared to extreme indexes - Tanzania, for example, where the average income does not exceed \$70. It is comical, grotesque, or tragic that, with the routine of seeing this tragedy, the gap that has grown during this period, from 30 to 100 times or 300, in its extremes, does not scandalize, does not revolt, is nothing more than a number.

Indeed, some complaints were heard and almost twenty years passed, so that the UN itself went back to sound a new alarm, louder, and were to point out, now even more difficult, that the inequalities are nastier in inhuman and inhuman in grotesque, as moreover, the villains were not ruthless and inhuman enough, tragic enough; we would have to say, in the appalling wickedness or simply tragic conditions of the world, to try to express what is happening".

In fact, the scandal denounced thirty years ago has only gotten worse, as has been analysed, and the trend is that it is getting worse and worse - having increased the gap between rich and poor, if we do not change the foundations of social organisation, starting with the current economic order or disorder, spread like dogma, and put into practice with the insensitivity of robots, or the repeated beating of the machine, because in this reductionism, everything is just numbers, until we realize that numbers hide humans, or the human process - and this is not a number.

The insensitivity of those who have the systems.

The UN denunciation, however, has not succeeded in getting the beneficiary Nations of the systems to create or indicate corrective mechanisms capable of generating concrete measures to reverse the process. On the contrary, one has the impression, and recent events confirm that the United Nations, to the extent that it denounces imbalances and integrates its action into the mass of consciousness in favour of change, moving away from the systems that concentrate and dominate the world, is turning into an embarrassing mechanism for the masters of the process and it is necessary to weaken it, rendering it powerless. The recent invasion of Iraq, in defiance of the UN, in obvious contempt of the world's conscience, and its repulsion, sometimes contained by fear or by the interplay of interests, is one of the clear signs of how law between nations, the evolution of the process, or the change of fundamental principles and existing structures does not interest those who have the systems.

We continue the analysis of "The Third Millennium Revolution":

Thus, the question of inequality continues to be more in the realm of moral issues, to be dealt with at congresses and symposia, or transferred to bodies that do not have mechanisms for direct intervention in the economic and financial order, or even in law or policy, and other bodies of various kinds - councils and committees, churches, etc. - so that everything remains as it is.

And concludes:

The beneficiaries of the current state of affairs are not concentrating their efforts and capacity to create alternative instruments and mechanisms. In reality, in their unconscious, they are not interested in changing the current social order in depth and the structures that benefit them. Driven by their survival instinct, they prefer small price corrections that prolong their privileges, allow them to survive; or the distribution of alms in the form of subsidiary financing, or direct subsidies whose sources, basically, come from mechanisms of aspiration on their own economies apparently benefited, ironically, through speculative applications. They also use bags or baskets of food, which, while prolonging life, weaken consciousness, and help maintain the state of injustice and exclusion.

1. 3. THE DIMENSION OF INEQUALITIES

While remedial action is lingering, the exclusion figures confirm the unsustainability of the process, if it continues in the current direction.

Growing gap that unbalances the system.

Back to the figures that are part of the tables and graphs in the - **REVOLUTIONS OF THE THIRD MILLENNIUM**, some of them already mentioned at the end of the previous part of this book. It is necessary to repeat or complete them, because they are essential data, and cannot simply go unnoticed. The following tables in the "**Third Millennium Revolution**" shows that less than 20% of the world's population concentrates more than 80% of the world's GDP - 82%, leaving, therefore, less than 20% of the GDP to more than 80% of the population and, in particular, only 14% for the 20%. Of the 80% of GDP concentrated, the largest share is in the hands of the United States and the countries of the European Union, where just over 10% of the world's population lives. Among these giants, competition is growing, seeking to overtake - or eliminate - a competitor. In essence, this explains the expansionism of the European Union and American interventionism. Meanwhile, China and Japan are continuing along alternative paths that will undoubtedly lead them to form one or two blocks of influence with 1/3 of the world's population. What remains are India, Brazil or Africa, the Arab world and Latin America, the most excluded world ...

I extract further figures and analysis from the "Third Millennium Revolution":

On the other hand, of the 20% of GDP in the hands of the excluded, only 5% is in the hands of 80% of this population, because in these countries the same concentration is repeated - and worsening: 20% of the population concentrates on average more than 90% of the GDP. This means that among the excluded, the numbers of concentration exceed the world average of exclusion. This fact is largely due to the strategy practiced in these countries - Brazil is a good example that, since it is impossible to take everyone to the first world, we take some - the privileged system, to the circle of developed countries. Concentration must, therefore, be higher, and with higher concentration there is greater exclusion. Hence the exorbitant profits of the financial systems, or mega-corporations, transnational or not - in particularly those related to basic infrastructure - structure, the computer, telecommunications and oil industries, and speculation in general. Meanwhile ... slums, exclusion, unemployment...

The ineffectiveness of the strategy, which only widens the gap and dangerously increases the imbalances, is not perceived. In Brazil, it has been practiced for at least 40 years, and despite the absolute primacy of the economy, of the celebrated economic policy, the country has gone from being the 9th or 10th largest economy in the world to becoming the 15th, walking backwards. Meanwhile, there is increasing concentration, increasing power, increasing policing around the world.

Brazilian inequality is thus a perfect example of the consequences of the application of this ambiguous strategy that has been practiced for almost half a century, at least since 1964 in Brazil, and which dominates the process. Thus, nothing has changed in the essence of the strategy, through regime change, from military rule to self-styled social democracy, or from the latter to the recently launched era - which could be called populist voluntarism - of the rise of the Workers' Party to power. Without an alternative project that is truly national and, on the contrary, committed to maintaining the system, the claim is made to keep the contradictory systems alive: concentration producing exclusion, with social compassion producing welfare rather than favouring the expected and promised synthesis. Thus, it perpetuates and aggravates the contradiction, instead of taking a step towards this synthesis.

As a result, social inequalities continue to grow. Profits from the banking system in 2003 were close to $20 billion, and from a single infrastructure company - Oil, $17 billion. This means that only these segments made a profit this year of about 30% of what the state has available for investment, once the almost $150 billion of debt is deducted, mainly due to financial speculation, half of which is guaranteed by the primary surplus, used more to maintain speculative systems, or the debt charges, which are in fact immortalized by transforming the primary surplus into a bonus to be recovered later on rather than to repay the debt itself.

Therefore, the strategy is assumed that it is necessary to maintain these indices in order to be credible in the international market, to ensure the entry of resources that generate the financial balance promised to these same systems. Society is out of this circle - no matter what happens with it.

We have to get back to questions they can't keep quiet about:

- What credibility does this have, at the price of excluding millions of human beings from access not only to the benefits of development, but to the fundamental rights of citizenship, or the human condition: income, employment, health, housing, education, finally, the fundamental right to participate in the process itself?

- What credibility does it have that depends on the mood of the stock exchanges or markets, led by the analysts of the speculative systems?

- How credible is this credibility, which is dictated by the Morgan Agency, by its market analysts, or by others, explicit representatives of speculative systems?

- What credibility is this which is granted or withdrawn according to the evaluation of this origin and inspiration, whatever the real conditions of the country, its real situation as a society, a gesture similar to removing the ladder, leaving the painter hanging from the brush?

- What kind of sovereignty - guaranteed and presupposed, again, of the dignity and freedom of a people condemned to depend on the injection of liquidity, often its own money, the fruit of speculation, exercised over it, which controls the systems?

To argue that the consequences or the threat of a collapse of the financial system would be unimaginable is to ignore the greatest threat posed by the disintegration or decay of society.

It must be said that the dichotomy between averting risk by adhering to the system or compromising the process is a false dilemma, as if there were no other solutions, a statement that is constantly repeated.

However, there are alternatives, starting with the effort to create, or at least extend, reliability criteria, which cannot be limited to financial interests. Any country's risk, or Brazil's reliability, cannot be reduced to its commitment to generate financial resources for guarantee speculative profits and accept exorbitant costs to the detriment of its viability as a society or as a nation. It means taking a much greater risk.

Indicators such as natural resources, population, political and national will, competence, ethical commitment, participation and global cooperation, human development indices and others, could be criteria or indicators to be put on the table of global processes and decisions, rather than quiet submission and unrestricted obedience to financial criteria imposed by speculation.

But to do so, we need to be aware of alternative indicators. To this end, we must create the necessary conditions so that, thanks to these indicators, quality investments can be guaranteed, replacing the easy and reductive criterion of primary surplus, which only guarantees speculation, at the price of consolidating the state of misery of an ever-growing section of society.

Why does it seem inevitable to maintain the comfortable position that there are no alternatives to considering economic policy, or, what is worse, financial or monetary policy, as the supreme value and guarantee of sustainability? How can we explain that, in spite of this, without any significant progress in the social field, the Brazilian economy has fallen from 9th or 10th position in the ranking of the world's largest economies to 15th position?

I extract from "**The Third Millennium Revolution**", the graph showing the size of the inequalities - or the unequal distribution of income in Brazil, the consequence of this option to take a few to the first world, to balance the finances at the price of exclusion from society and mankind. The graph compares the poor distribution of Brazilian income with the distribution of income in other countries; even countries much less developed than Brazil.

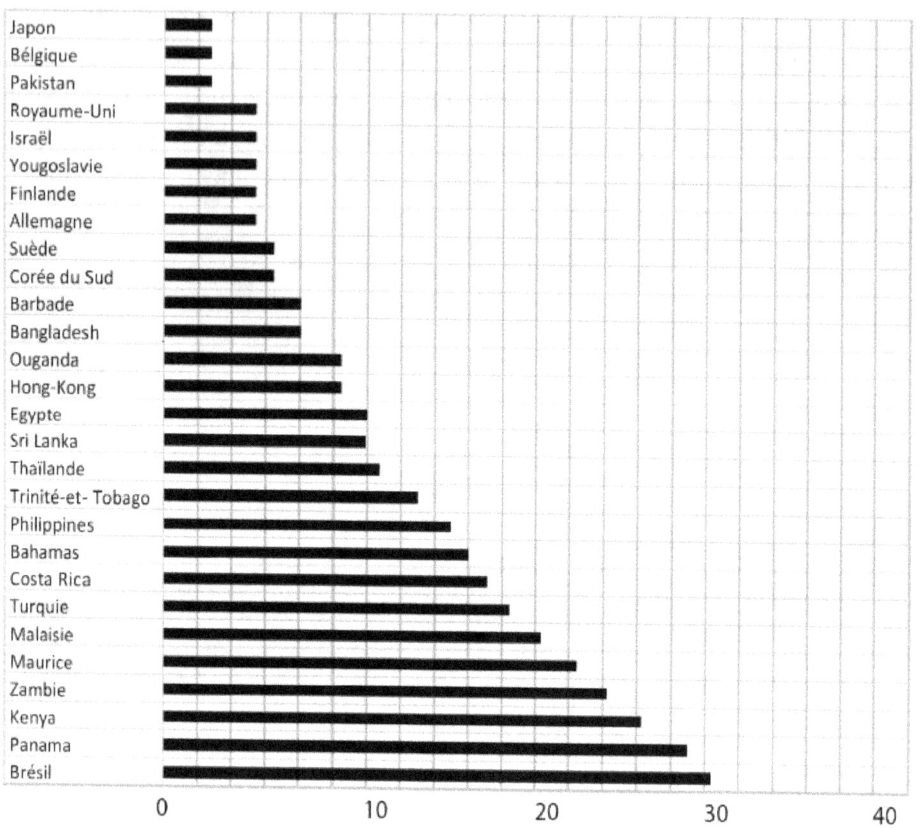

At one point, "The Third Millennium Revolution" presents a second picture, which shows the extremely unequal way in which this wealth is distributed among several countries. This table shows how the poor distribution of wealth, a consequence of the process of concentration and exclusion, occurs globally, at the global level. The inequality figures extend to the comparison that can be made between developed, underdeveloped and developing countries.

Table No. 1 - Participation of some developed and non-developed countries in world GDP in relation to their respective populations

	POPULATION IN 1000	GDP IN BILLION DOLLARS	% OF WORLD POPULATION	% OF WORLD GDP
Brazil	160,000	800	2.7	3.2
USA	280,000	7,200	4.7	28.8
India	900,000	342	15.0	1.3
France	65,000	1,540	0.9	6.1
South Africa	42,000	134	0.7	0.5
England	58,000	953	0.9	3.8
Tanzania	116,000	276	1.9	1.0
China	1,200,000	662	20.0	2.6
Nigeria	115,000	64	1.9	0.25
Germany	80,000	2,450	1.3	9.0
Japan	125,000	4,800	0.2	10.0

In the table, we see that the percentage concerning the participation to GDP versus population is very unequal, for example in the United States[20], in Germany and Japan, in contrast to countries such as India, China, the Nigeria or Brazil.

This would be the case if there was no population growth. If, however, US GDP were to grow by 4%, the increase in US GDP would exceed $300 billion, which would mean that each American would earn more than $1,000 on their own income.

I am referring to the situation in Brazil, according to recently published data, again relating it to U.S. growth in the first quarter of 2004 - real data.

---

[20] According to current estimates, US GDP has already surpassed $9 billion.
The average rate of growth in developed countries has been in the order of 3 or 4%, which is a very high level adds billions of dollars to the GDP of these countries every year. However, as great that the percentage of GDP growth in China, for example, may be, proportionally, the volume of wealth added for a population that is growing proportionally to the population of the country is less than the growth of wealth in the United States, or in developed countries, even though their GDP is growing at lower rates and their population is not growing much. By way of comparison, hypothetically, if China's GDP growth is 10%, the wealth of the country would be available for the 1.3 billion Chinese will be around $66 billion, which means that every Chinese person will get an extra $55.

Brazil received euphoric news that it would have grown by more than 2% this quarter. The US was up about 4%. This means that every Brazilian, not counting the population growth that would reduce the rate to almost zero, will have an increase in income of the highest order of 70 dollars, while every American will have increased by almost 20 times - in the order of 1300 US dollars. This is how the gap is growing and the imbalance is growing, even considering the small advances of the excluded.

Extreme rates of income inequality.

Subsequently, The Third Millennium Revolution will analyse the different aspects of inequality in many countries. The analysis says:

From this perspective, the rigorous denunciation of the UN report continues, revealing the figures of concentration and exclusion.
Of the 23 trillion dollars that make up the world's GDP, only 5 trillion are held by underdeveloped or developing countries, while 18 trillion are generated and held by developed countries, according to the report. However, the so-called developing countries, most of them without any development, comprise more than 80% of the world's population, or just over 4.8 billion people, while in the developed countries the total population is about 1 billion.

The per capita ratio in the developed countries is 1:15, while in the so-called developing countries it is barely 1:1. To make matters worse, it should also be borne in mind that this disparity is only an apparent disparity, being an average disparity, and the average conceals the extreme imbalance of concentration and exclusion in the countries themselves, which is much more serious and much more unjust, when analysing the internal structure of the distribution of wealth that gives rise to this average.

In line with this analysis, the UN report examines the structure of domestic income in different countries. Here are a few cases;

-       *In the United States, for example, where the average income today is $24,000, the average income of the poorest population group, considered as 23% of the total population, is about $5,000, i.e. at levels equivalent to the Brazilian average income. Imagine the income of the richest strata, in the*

United States, so that, despite the poorest, we arrive at the average income of $24,000!

-   Brazil, which has an average income of around $5,370, the poorest parcel of land, considered as 10.5% of the economically active population (a concept to avoid reaching the extremely excluded or those with no income, strata totaling almost 50% of what this population could be) has a per capita income of around $560, i.e. an income equivalent to the average income of Tanzania - returning to the country already mentioned, which is, for its part, $580. In Tanzania, however, the average income of the poorest segment of the population falls to $70, again without taking into account the extremely excluded population.

We must repeat and emphasize, however, that when we talk, in Brazil and Tanzania, about the average income of the poorest population, we do not consider the enormous part of the population that simply has no income, nor do we identify those plots whose income pushes the average down, and which, as a whole, constitutes the majority of the population".

These figures and this analysis is a sample of what is happening in the world. I conclude, again quoting **THE THIRD MILLENNIUM REVOLUTION**:

It is on this scale that opulence becomes unjust and exclusion becomes inhuman. Unjustly inhuman or tragi-comic, if more could be said, in order to awaken and open the eyes of those who can still see, on the direction that is given to the process. Income disparity results in disparity in consumption, another significant indicator of how people live, how they participate in, or are excluded from, the goods produced by development.

Given the differences between the richest layer in the first world, which pulls up the average income of $25,000 or more, and the poorest in Tanzania, for example, which pulls down the average income of $70, if we want to understand why the difference in income of 30 or 100 times between the richest and the poorest now exceeds 300 times. That is the situation the process has reached at the end of this century. The inequality which, while unjust, has become inhuman, or grotesque during this period, continues to grow dramatically, widening indefinitely the gap between rich and poor and increasing global imbalance".

The Third Millennium Revolution makes the analysis of consumption inequalities that I am transcribing:

Inequality of access to consumption.

From a consumption point of view, the gap falls to impressive levels, even for so-called inelastic products like food - as if someone's stomach is 20 times higher than others - which would be biologically monstrous. We only realize that in sociology, or in politics, we also produce monstrosities.

The own graph printed on the cover of the Human Development Report, UN 1998 - Brazilian edition, shows several indicators of consumption in developed and developing countries. The consumption rates of underdeveloped countries are represented by simple blocks in the foreground. We see the "unfair" disparity, which is obvious, and we now notice that the imbalance in consumption mirrors the imbalances in production and income.

Chart No. 2 - Global Gaps: Consumption Indicators.

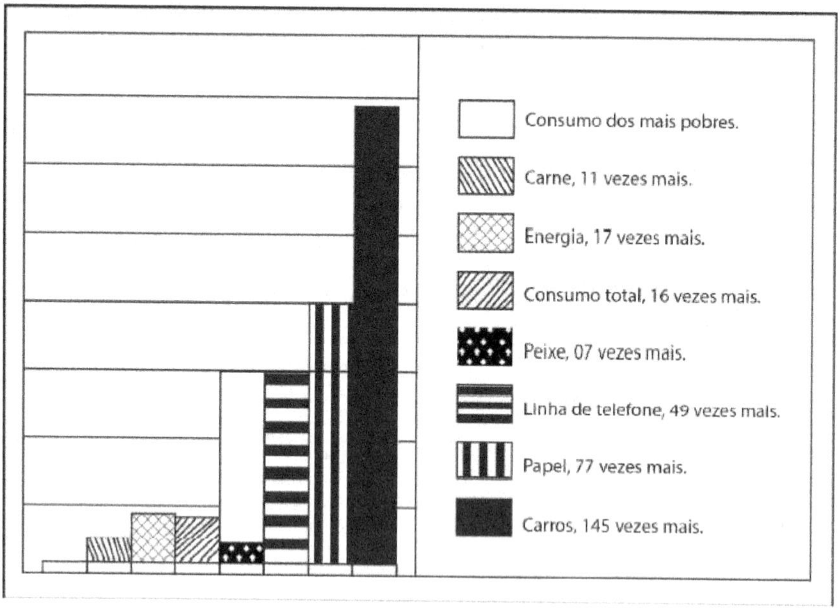

Source: UNDP - Human Development Report - 1998.

This analysis, therefore, verifies that the dimension of inequalities that occur between countries, within each country, in both the developed and developing world, or in the third world, is proportionate. Or, alternatively, in production, income and consumption. Nothing escapes the global imbalance that is increasing, thus aggravating the path of rupture.

Where will the process take us in case it isn't reversed?

The inevitable consequences of the principles of competition and concentration, brought to the post-technological world, produce the imbalance and unsustainability of the process, inevitably and irreversibly. As long as these fundamental principles continue to inspire the organization and functioning of society, in its multiple aspects, there is no chance of reversing the path towards rupture, and building a harmonious and sustainable society, or a safe or humane minimum.

In fact, at an ever-increasing rate, the gap between rich and poor - countries and people - is widening, and the process shows that it is an illusion to claim that concentrated growth will eventually be reversed globally, for all. This might perhaps be true if it were a static phenomenon, not a process.

But this is a dynamic phenomenon - an extremely dynamic process. In this process, if there were to be a backflow, it would always be out of phase, and that out of phase would cause the gap to widen every day, but at different stages than in the previous stages. It may even reach a higher stage. But that is not the point.

The fact is that the imbalance, or the gap, will always be greater and can have more serious consequences precisely for this reason: being at a higher stage, it confronts and moves consciences in a more acute way and, for this very reason, it becomes more and more serious. This is the tragedy, or dehumanization, or injustice, or the grotesqueness of the process, or its unsustainability on the path that leads to its rupture, if it is not reversed in time.

Some figures and considerations from the ILO.

Participation, income and work are inseparable concepts. Moreover, the definition adopted in **The Age of Man** has already become a classic, affirming that work is the form through which the economy takes on its full social dimension. **The**

ILO - International Labour Organization, has long denounced the deterioration of working conditions in the world, and some of these denunciations have already been commented on.

Comparing income data with the labour market situation, where millions of people are being pushed out of the labour market, will allow us to delve deeper into the reasons for the process of imbalance that we are experiencing.

It must be seen that exclusion from the labour market is reaching, at an ever-increasing speed, a larger part of the world's population - and thus preventing their participation in income, well-being or the benefits of development, i.e. in promoting the humanization of the economy. This is happening in a context where averages, figures, the market and speculation continue to prevail, ever more distant from human rights or the promotion of human development. Exclusion therefore takes precedence over participation.

"The number of unfortunate people, and those living in sub-human conditions, continues to grow, as long as the magic of accounting and econometric equations is applied and developed," continues **The Third Millennium Revolution**, which analyses the ILO figures and which I am transcribing again.

The figures are now taken from ILO - International Labour Organization studies presented at the 2nd Conference on Human Settlements (Habitat II) in Istanbul in July 1996. These figures show that one third of the world's urban population (estimated at 1.5 billion people), i.e. 500 million people, at the beginning of this decade (1990s) lived in poverty. This number, according to the study, could reach one billion by the year 2000, nearly 50% of the same population at the turn of the century. The number of very poor people tends to increase further in the entry of the

Millennium, if the parameters of the process are not changed, or if the foundations governing the world organization allow the process to continue. The year 2000 has arrived, and the process shows no sign of change. The current figures for the world population, and not only for the urban population, indicate that about 2 billion people live below the conditions of poverty, with less than 2 dollars a day to survive.

In reality, the ILO figures relate only to the urban population of the world, when we know that many, perhaps the largest and most wretched part of the population, hide in the lost corners of countries without statistics, in the vast interior of lost and forgotten rural areas, a concept which, moreover, is losing its meaning for many regions because, on the one hand, urban centers attract, and on the other hand they spread their problems and dramas, without being able to spread their benefits.

For all this, the number of very poor people continues to grow and will grow even more, because population growth will raise the world's population to nearly 10 billion people in the first half of the next century. This growth will take place in the underdeveloped countries - in Asia, Africa, South America, and will stabilize in the developed countries - and this has already been analyzed.

The imbalance will therefore continue to grow.

It's impossible not to wonder again:

How long will the process continue to be sustainable? Or are we doomed to let the balance push to the breaking point?

An Alternative Analysis of "The Revolution of the Third Millennium".

The process of exclusion thus worsens, with a global growth in unemployment; The Third Millennium Revolution deepens the analysis of the issue of global imbalances, linking it directly to that of employment. In reality, work is the way in which people generate income and, through it, they participate in the process, assuming and exercising their dignity, because it is the income that gives them the conditions to ensure, freely, in addition to providing for their own needs, their own development - material, cultural, spiritual, "by the sweat of their brow", a slight allusion to the ethical (biblical) basis of the question.

I'll take the transcript of this analysis:

"At the same time, unemployment has risen, both in developed and developing countries. In developed countries, the number of unemployed is

increasing mainly due to the automation of processes and services in pursuit of productivity, competitiveness, profit, or simply convenience. These advances, however, are not accompanied by an equivalent rate of offer of another job, or by a preparation of people for the exercise of new functions that are more intelligent, less automatable, or adapted to meet the quests for well-being or quality of life, sectors that are growing and expanding more and more in the post-technological era, and where it is essential to maintain, even if only as a sign of significant participation, the human presence or touch".

Progress will not be accompanied by structures and mechanisms to use new technologies for the liberation of man from traditional working methods. I would like to remind you once again that, even in the post-technological age, work will continue to be a presupposition and to give meaning to the life of the human species, but in new forms and formats adapted to new forms of occupation. In this new era of increasing complexity, of globalism, work, in the most varied forms, will seek leisure, intellectual, cultural and spiritual development, i.e. forms corresponding to a greater blossoming of the being and quality of human life. In this sense, technology will also be oriented, as a cause and as a corollary, at the service of this search, at the service of man, rather than being only at the service of what can concentrate more or of the deification of money, profit and power, or of the alienating search for things, destroying the harmony or balance necessary for social organization, for the life of people and for the sustainability of the process.

The analysis continues in **The Third Millennium Revolution** :

In this context, even in the developed countries - in the past considered as full employment, the number of unemployed already exceeded the 50 million mark at the end of the last decade (the 1980s), reaching its peak in several countries, approaching, in a localized manner, 10% of the active population. Extensive social programs, maintained with the budget that concentrated wealth provides to the first world, have made up for the shortfalls by offering social assistance to the unemployed who often find themselves, despite this assistance, producing anti-social ghettos, losing value, leading them to dependency and all forms of degradation and violence. This reaction can be considered normal, or inevitable, because idleness and assistance do not represent man's natural condition, but rather work and self-fulfillment.

The situation in the ghettos is aggravated by the immigration of the poor, or agitated by violence in different parts of the world, creating new imbalances and provoking new conflicts. The same blindness that keeps entire continents in an inhuman condition full of misery, therefore specifically affects large sectors of the beneficiaries of the system, despite the wealth they have accumulated.

However, it is in the excluded part of the world, despite its enormous potential, the exploitation of which, for centuries, has made the wealth of the most developed countries, this is where there are still huge reserves of human and natural resources, one of the alternatives for overcoming imbalances, if these resources are used sustainably in favour of the excluded themselves and not continue, as in the era of classical colonialism, to be exploited, often in a predatory manner, to meet the demands of new settlers - the new era of post-technological metropolises - or to absorb the survival needs of the excluded.

Africa, to take as an example the poorest continent, taking sustainable advantage of its natural resources, combined with the size of its territory, will be able to absorb twice as many people - perhaps a number equivalent to those dying from malnutrition and inhuman conditions, if it takes advantage of its natural resources. It so happens that the history of Africa has been, and continues in its new forms, stained by colonialism, slavery and the predatory exploitation of its natural resources and its people, the main responsibility of the countries that today concentrate the world's wealth, leaving the continent with a legacy of famine and disease that ravage entire populations in a genocide that in the future will demand accountability from this generation, just as the conscious part of this generation demands accountability from the genocides of the past.

The promoters and owners of the systems, those who manipulate the virtual and speculative economy, must assume their share of responsibility, regardless of the price, reasons, costs or limitation of their profits. This is a debt of the developed peoples, who, under the cover of colonization - and even Christianizing people, have devastated cultures, systems of life, and left people in poverty on long occupied territories.

It is also a requirement of humanity, in the name of ethics, history, civilization, or quite simply of its own survival.

However, the misperception of the systems that dominate the world, just capable of meeting the demands of the market, the fundamentalism of profit for which everything is sacrificed, takes precedence. The expansion of food production and its adequate trade or distribution in a hungry world is prevented or made impossible by the market, competition, profits, as well as preventing the production of welfare and the access of the excluded to products resulting from the process of change brought about by technology.

It is necessary for the developed world, so often eloquent in its criticism of the realities of the Third World, to first pay its debt to this world exploited previously by colonial regimes and now by the financial and commercial systems, in order to regain the morality necessary for criticism.

In this context, of the market, of the virtual and speculative economy and of profit, the pace of technological innovation is also not determined, it does not take into account human needs, collective needs, or the harmony and balance needed in society, or of individuals, individually. Technological innovation is driven solely by the interests of competition and concentration, of market domination, without adapting its pace and management to the needs of the survival of the process.

This does not represent a position contrary to innovation, but only a rationalisation of its use, in order to make technological innovation harmonious with the system to which it belongs, and not a restructuring factor that will lead it to break down.

Besides, this is a normal procedure used in all things.
Why not with the social process?

When the part of an engine is improved to the maximum, as long as the whole engine is not adapted to it, or as long as it does not adapt to the engine in order to work synchronously with it, it is impossible to insert it into the engine, because either it will not work, or if it does work, it will be able to make it explode. This, however, does not happen with technological innovation in the social process.

Once it is ready, it is inserted into society, without any concern about whether it works, or whether it explodes the social system. This is because the social process is subtler than mechanical systems, and its balances are less visible, so its sustainability seems less worrying.

The examples given show how the procedures and norms imposed on the functioning of the post-technological society, created in colonial times and stubbornly guarded, determine continued exclusion, with all its consequences, as if this order were a sustainable, ethical and legally acceptable system.

However, it is impossible not to take into account that the dominant power and its wealth originated largely, and is still maintained by the puncture exerted on the colonized world, yesterday and today, subject to the same, but now sophisticated, norms and procedures that have allowed them to continue to concentrate - now without limits - and the new colonialism, through the power of technology: the new technological colonialism, which is added to the commercial and financial systems, already mentioned.

There's nothing new in this insensitivity. Those who in the past promoted and maintained slavery, colonialism and other forms of exclusion also failed to realize the magnitude of the crime they practiced, just as those who today use technology to exclude the same piece of humanity and, by excluding it, continue to dominate the world. Either they were aware of it, but there were always reasons to silence consciences; or legislators; or judges; or those in power.

In addition to these matters of essential importance, there is another factor to be taken into account in statistics and analyses relating to working conditions. This is the manipulation of statistics - due to the variety of methods used, each often used at its own convenience. For example, monitoring the employment situation in terms of the ratio of job entries and exits represents little in terms of employment opportunities, given that only a small part of the working population (about 40% in Brazil) and an even smaller part (less than 30%) work in controllable conditions. Rather, the method reveals the state of the economy, in terms of its capacity to create jobs and generate income from work, which is something else.

Statistics, as has been said, serve to reveal the truth. But consciously or unconsciously manipulated or misused, statistics also serve to hide the truth. Inadequate methods, or statistics that are not transparent enough, hide the situation of millions of people who do not have access to work and income, are not relevant to the economy and, therefore, are not taken into account by the statistics. However, these people do exist, they are human beings. They are outside the economy, but they are part of society, form society, and society should care about them before it cares about the economy. Although they do not, in fact, belong to the economically active population - which is an economic concept - these people are unemployed in the strict sense, even though they have never entered or left the labour market, or have never belonged to categories that the economy characterizes. Those segments of the population that are not recorded in the statistics often belong, however, to the most excluded category, thus increasing imbalances.

The Brazilian case.

In this context, I analyse the case of Brazil, through the table in paragraph 2. Analysis of the table shows very different figures of 6% or 7% unemployment, often obtained by the process of recording the difference between dismissals and admissions to formal employment, or even 17% or 18% unemployment in some large cities, obtained by other methods, such as direct search, or at home, which are closer to reality. It so happens that these figures are taken from the simple difference between those who leave and those who enter the market, or who, after having produced some form of income, have stopped producing. The latter consider those who have neither joined nor left the labour market, but who, in some way, have produced income. These belong to the labour force and are counted. But neither considers those who have never entered the market or who have been excluded from it without any registration or payment, those who constitute the extreme layer of social exclusion.

The table shows, first of all, that in Brazil, the working-age population is much higher than the economically active population (EAP). There are more than 100 million people of working age. However, the labor force - which has been identified as having a certain type of income, constitutes only 76 million people, which is only 71% of the working age population. Where are the rest, nearly 30 million people, or even if they are not considered, students, pensioners and others who are in this age group, an amount greater than about 20% of the working-age population?

And it should be noted that we are talking about the working-age population, not the total population.

Looking at the PEA (economically active population), it will be easy to see that only 29 million people (out of 76 million) work in the formal economy, characterized in Brazil by the "signed work card". This represents only 38% of the PEA. The rest is made up of self-employed owners and workers (16 million) and workers in the informal sector - thus generating some form of income, a type of activity that can range from the offender to the waste collector, the street vendor or the car "keeper", in the streets or public squares.

Finally, there is the issue of the unemployed in the formal market. These can vary in percentage from about 3% to 4% of the total population, or up to 19% of their category (with a formal contract).

If, however, we consider the unemployed, those who are not in the formal sector or are not part of the AEO - but are of working age, who consume, who have the right to life in decent human conditions, we reach the alarming figures of 35% of the total population, 41% of the population of working age, or 53% of the economically active population.

If we add the 19% of the working-age population who do not work at all to those who may be working in the informal market - also about 19% of the total population, and the unemployed in the formal sector, about 6%, we arrive at an index of inactive people above 40% of the working-age population. This is unemployment in disguise.

Table No. 2 - Structure of the Brazilian Population in Relation to the Labor Market (*).

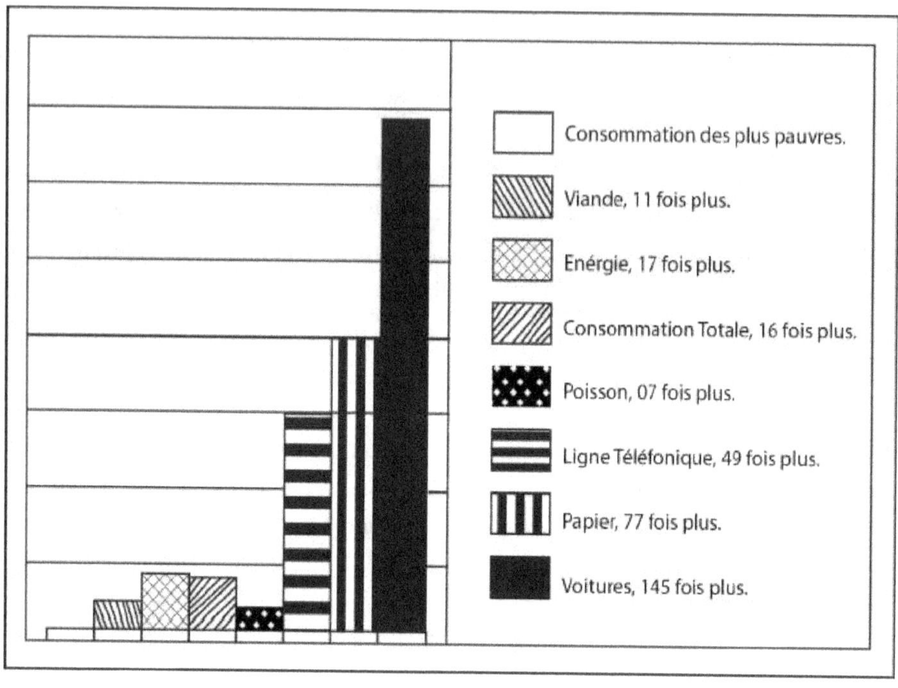

Table No. 02 - The real labor and unemployment situation in Brazil.

Indicator	Absolute No. in millions	% of total population	% of the respective category
1. Total population	160.0	-	-
2. Population of working age (between 15 and 60 years)	103.0	64.0	-
3. AEP identified	76.0	47.0	71.0
3.1 With registration on the work card	29.0	18.0	38.0
3.1.1 Unemployed	5.7	3.5	19.0
3.2 Proprietary and autonomous	16.0	10.0	21.0
3.3 In the informal market	31.0	19.0	40.0
4. Economically inactive non-employed working age population	27.0	15.0	-
4.1 Students	3.0	1.8	2.9
4.2 Retirees	4.0	2.0	3.8
4.3 Inactive	20.0	12.7	19.0
4.4 Inactive and unemployed population (*)	25.7	16.0	24.0
5 - Population inactive, unemployed and on the informal market.	56.7	35.4 53.00 (PEA)	41.00 (AIP)

(*) The figures for the end of the 1990s are approximate, as some of the criteria used differ from the official tables, and they themselves differ from each other. Their evolution towards more current - less consolidated - numbers, does not change the analysis or the processes.

This enormous population mass, excluded from production systems, does not participate in social life, work, living conditions in their human dimension.

This number is a better reflection of reality than the statistics usually shown and commented on in the media or in official circles. Figures that estimate between 40% and 60% of the population living below the poverty line are also more realistic.

This eye-destroying level - and consciences - are everywhere in cities and their suburbs, in slums and in the countryside. Figures and statistics, which are not adequately explained or are often manipulated by marketing, are an incentive to make mistakes, with serious consequences for society, and permanent errors for public policy and business decisions. Official sources or statistics sow confusion in society before its optimism that contrasts with visible reality.

The long analysis of the Brazilian case reflects what is happening in the world, especially in the excluded world, as concentration increases, unbalancing the social structure - pushing it towards a certain form of rupture.

About a third of Brazil's population, something approaching 60 million people, lives more or less in conditions of exclusion. Extrapolating this number to a third of the planet's population, it is more than the 2 billion people, denounced by official reports, living below the poverty line or something close to it, not counting those living in the developed world. This number, as we have seen, is constantly growing, not least because the population is growing much more among the excluded than in the world that has benefited from concentration.

This is an example, the example of Brazil, which represents a good sample - an average between the best and worst situations that occur in the non-developed world, which reaches 2/3 of the world's population, without great prospects.

Let's get back to the questions that can't be killed:

Where is the security and sustainability of a model that produces such imbalances? How many steps away from a break if we are not able to reverse the process in time? What price can the future pay if the imbalances continue to grow and the process, or the current model, concentrates and excludes?

The ghettos of the outcasts and the walls of Jericho.

At the same time, the ghettos of the excluded are forming, and the masters of the systems are building walls around them to defend themselves against the world around them. To no avail. They act like the people of Jericho.

In nature, no imbalance lasts for a long time, and this is a universal law, which applies as much to things as to living beings, and to the world of psychology or the spirit, to the whole universe at last, and thus to man and societies.

This is why the consequences of imbalances built into human processes, and not corrected in time, are inevitable. Insecurity, which constitutes itself as a mark of these times, which could be times of change, or of organized evolution, affects individuals, society, as much as nations and states, weak or powerful, as far as they seem unattainable, the powerful. The insecurity that affects the world, is not a cyclical problem, which can be contained by weapons, by medical or psychological progress or the wealth of nations and is concentrated in the hands of those who dominate the world and imagine that they control the world. In reality, it must be realized that insecurity is a consequence of specific causes, which cause it to be reborn everywhere in the same or different forms and with a vigour as great or greater than the repression or control that the masters of the systems claim to exercise over it. Only the elimination of structural imbalances - the causes that give rise to it - is capable of eliminating insecurity.

Otherwise, the systems, once again, will behave like the people of Jericho, who, in order to feel safe, have built walls around the city.

Neither weapons nor cannon were needed to destroy the walls that had been built, and the sense of security that they inspired.

The Jewish people began to march around the city and raise their prayer to Jeovah.

On the seventh day the people cried out in unison, and the walls of Jericho fell down, as if they were walls of paper.

Placing this history in the present context, it is impossible not to detect the cry of the people of Israel in the mass of consciousness that is forming around the world, while we can approach the seventh day, the day of the rupture, if the process of concentration and exclusion is not reversed.

2.   THE PLANET MUST BE SAVED

The destruction of the Earth and the role of technology.

It is estimated that in the last hundred years, that is, since the regime of maximum production, competition and absolute use of technology was adopted - also with a possible justification to meet the demands of the population explosion - the planet has been destroyed to a greater extent than it has already been destroyed in the entire history of its occupation by the human species.

About 30% of the Earth's resources have already been depleted. No problem if people don't think about the next hundred years, the next thousand years and the future of humanity, the generations to come. No problem if this future doesn't exist and everything ends with this generation.

There are also those who avoid the question, thinking that technology will provide the answers to the problems of the future. Faith can even be a beautiful answer, and many believe blindly in their new gods.

But reality does not reinforce this belief. If this were so, technology would not have allowed the said 30% of the earth's resources to be destroyed in such a short period of time.

The reality is that technology, despite the speed of innovation that produces it, has not prevented the destruction of the planet.

Instead, it has contributed to the rate of destruction becoming faster every day.

It is fair to think that technology could be used to replace the use of non-renewable natural resources with renewable resources. It is also true that technology could introduce non-destructive processes of natural resources, or less polluting ones, to save the planet. Technology could even produce instruments and forms, unimaginable today except in the realm of fiction.

It may be a path, but it is not very rational to hand over the future of humanity to it, especially if we consider that it is a dynamic process, the coordination of which, as a result, will have to be continuous and as rapid as innovation. But this has not been the case so far.

As long as in this context of competition and concentration, controlling the process, technology will be used to produce and sophisticate with billions or trillions of dollars, the war industry and the alliance of the war industry with business and speculation, or the financial exploitation of the world; as long as the dominant policy gives priority to business, economics, interests and profits at any cost, or if technology is used or allowed to be used without limits for this purpose, even at the expense of the destruction of the planet, this is a dead end.

There are two sectors that dominate the process - the war industry and business, which show that faith in technology as the guardian of the Planet's salvation, without the necessary paradigm shifts, has no basis in reality.

The global policy of oil use, preventing in particular the development and adoption of various forms of bioenergy and renewable energies, the refusal to sign the Kyoto Protocol by the United States and other instruments to control the destruction of the planet are the most obvious examples that technology can hardly be expected to be a tool to save it, as long as the system-controlled model of competition and concentration survives.

It can be said, on the contrary, that the change in the use of technology in favour of the salvation of the earth, depends on the change of the current model in its various aspects: of consciousness, first; of concepts, second; of strategies and instruments, in short, which would mean a real revolution - the revolution that is proposed: The Third Millennium Revolution.

A change in this model, redirecting resources from war, competition and business to research, development and the adoption of technologies that respect the earth's resources and eliminate polluting and destructive methods and processes with the same priority and with volumes of the same size as those used in the current model and for its maintenance would give consistency to this alternative.

Through this understanding and these perspectives, transformed into comprehensive policies, this path would be possible. Once possible, technology could be an essential instrument for civilizational change, and for post-technical social organization - the new civilization.

If this does not happen and if the current social organization continues, the current model, after having restructured and dehumanized society, the planet will be destroyed and dehumanized - home and dwelling of men, made uninhabitable.

The answer, from this threat, moves into the realm of fiction.

Threats to destroy Earth.

The threat of destruction of the planet is not limited to a sector, a resource, or an area.

Initially the unconsciousness and today the madness of men - because it is impossible to affirm that we do not know what is happening and its consequences, leads the threat of destruction of the earth to the limits, wherever its presence has arrived, which is paradoxical, given that man is the conscience of the earth or the universe, as has already been affirmed on several occasions.

Or is he not the conscience of the universe? Those who have a small view of man will immediately say that he is not. Those who are afraid to admit that man has such a dimension will also tend to say no. The others, those who remain in debt with creation, will continue to seek, and will assume their supplement in faith, as Saint Thomas Aquinas teaches.

This is how the threat of destruction reaches the surface of the earth, its soil, its living canopy, the maritime and continental waters, the air, the atmosphere, and, who knows, begins to penetrate space, through the fury of man's unreasonable and erroneous ambitions, bringing death and destruction in its wake, rather than construction and life, i.e. primacy instead of civilization.

Pollution is taking over the Earth, and continues to increase dangerously.

Industrial and domestic discharges caused by industrial and agricultural processes without sufficient or adequate self or public controls, and the overpopulation of megacities - swollen cities - are destroying soil and water.

Although the Kyoto Protocol, which strengthened the commitment of 178 countries to reduce global pollution, carbon emissions, which are responsible for major climate change and global warming, increased by 10% after the protocol. In the United States, which is responsible for the largest share of carbon emissions and which, under the Bush administration, refused to sign the protocol, carbon emissions increased by 18%.

The hole in the ozone layer is one of the known effects of carbon emissions. The hole is growing steadily, leading to the question of pollution in the atmosphere.

UN technicians, however, denounce, also and above all, since the Johannesburg conference - Rio + 10, the cloud of pollutants, made up of carbon particles, organic sulphates and ashes, extends with an average thickness of 3 km over South Asia, from Japan to Afghanistan, from the north of China to Indonesia - an area equivalent to three times the Brazilian territory. The cloud retains about 15% of the sunlight.

According to the report, food harvests - with rice as the benchmark - have declined by about 10 percent; 500 million people die each year from respiratory problems.

-       The Asian cloud is not alone - and it can move quickly, affecting other parts of the globe. Similar phenomena occur in other parts of the world. They have also occurred over large cities such as São Paulo in Brazil, Mexico City in Mexico, and others, causing the so-called "thermal inversion" and other ailments.

-       The hole in the ozone layer, responsible for the melting of the southern polar ice cap - also at an increasing rate, combining with clouds of pollution, is producing climate change which, by increasing soil desertification, is producing global warming, amplifying periods of drought and determining the lack of control over rainfall patterns. The floods that have devastated parts of China, India and Bangladesh, in particular, may be another serious consequence.

-       It is estimated that 30% of continental waters have disappeared in the last 70 years, and the rest are threatened by pollution on an increasing scale - in cities, from industrial and domestic discharges, as we have seen. In rural areas, through the use of pesticides.

-       Rivers discharge polluted water into the sea, adding to the pollution produced by the coastal population, shipping and port movements. These effects, added to the atmospheric effects, begin to destroy marine life. It is estimated that

30% of coral reefs - the sanctuaries, or cradles of marine life, are in danger of disappearing.

- Planet Earth, once covered with immense forests, is turning into a huge desert, and only a few patches of forest resist, the Amazon in Brazil being the most expressive of them.

However, what remains - including the Amazon - is threatened with extinction. Only in the last decade of the last century - the 1990s - about 90 million hectares of forests worldwide were destroyed - the equivalent of something like 1/3 of the Amazon rainforest. Much of this destruction has also taken place in the Amazon, without there being a consistent program of research, occupation and sustainable use of this immense area by the government or by world society, which is claiming for the preservation of the Amazon.

- With the forests, with the water, with the seas, with the increasingly deteriorating atmosphere, are repeated in relation to the planet the imbalances that prevent the continuation of the human process, if this model is not modified, leading to the process of rupture. The price to be paid in this case will be unimaginable.

However, of all of the above, which is not catastrophic, but which represents the reality that surrounds us, or the process we are embarked upon, the most serious thing is that all of this has happened in less than a century. That is why the studies of responsible bodies such as WWF - World Wildlife Fund, among others, are right to draw attention to the conditions limiting the planet's capacity to bear, for more generations, the occupation of the Earth in the way it is happening.

We would be doomed to rapid extinction unless paradigms are changed, as proposed by UNESCO at the end of the World Conference on Sustainable Development, Rio 92:

"Each generation must leave the resources of water, soil and air as pure and unpolluted as when they first appeared on earth. Each generation owes its descendants the same quantity of animal species it has found"; or Gandhi's warning, addressed to his country - India, but which deserves to be meditated upon as a global warning:

"May God never allow India to adopt Western-style industrialization. England needs half of the planet's resources to achieve prosperity ("the empire on which the sun never sets!!!"). How many planets would a large country like India need? "

How many planets would the world need to destroy if it continued to maintain the model of competition, concentration and exclusion, to which it now insists on adding global deterioration, if the model is not changed?

But there is only one planet, and even if we imagine conquering other planets, we cannot do so by leaving behind us - again, a trail of death and destruction instead of building and life.

3.   SURVIVAL STRATEGIES

The proposals of the Developed.

Those who command the systems, the beneficiaries of the concentration model, and those who follow them, even those excluded from the systems, imagine, however, that they can survive by inserting small advances into the current model. In reality, these proposals are aimed at, or serve rather to maintain the model than to transform it. Tomasi di Lampedusa's teaching is perfectly practiced when he says that **everything must change so that nothing changes**. So he has disciples, the Italian "philosopher".

The book **The Third Millennium Revolution** makes a brief analysis of these strategies, all suggested by the first world - the world that maintains the current model, seeming to prove Skidmore, the "Brazilian", right in an interview with Vcja magazine.

I transcribe, in note[21] with the comments of the **Third Millennium Revolution**, the observations of Skidmore, and then some **strategies proposed by the Developed.**

---

[21] 21 "Thomas Skidmore, the dean of "Brazilian" refers to this difficulty by noting a certain "intellectual vacuum" in Brazil, in a recent interview with Veja Magazine (Ed. No. 1645). After quoting President Fernando Henrique Cardoso, according to whom "there is no alternative to our economic policy *" (the argument, moreover, defended and repeated by his opponents then and now in power), the Brazilian continued: "There are this general feeling in Brazil, as well as

After examining some of these proposals, the oldest, such as those presented by the Club of Rome, or by the Trilateral, in the middle of the last century, the Third Millennium Revolution examines some of the most current, so-called reformist, trends.

I transcribe:

- Liberalism, neo-liberalism and the Third Way.

Liberalism, neo-liberalism and the Third Way are in this perspective.

Historically, liberalism has left the regulation of social relations, particularly economic relations, to the market, with a minimum of state intervention. Recently, in England, Margaret Thatcher and in the United States, Ronald Reagan have been the maximum expressions of this proposal, proving to be positive, momentarily, for developed countries: freedom to concentrate, to penetrate the weakest economies and to puncture them, but extremely perverse for the excluded - with no limits to exclude.

Unlimited liberalism, as it could not fail to be, has ended up increasing poverty and imbalances, not only in the undeveloped world, but in the rich countries themselves, in the United States and Great Britain as examples where economic growth has not approached the poverty line, and where state welfare has not prevented the growth of those excluded and marginalized from the system - reduced to their ghettos or increasingly pushed to exclusion in their own regimes of abundance where they live, and partly transformed into a parcel of the mass of consciousness that develops, opposes and descends into the streets.

In line with the government's extensive social programs and responsibility, particularly in the areas of education, health, employment and social

---

in other developing countries, that there is only one right policy. That's the policy coming out of Washington. We are not looking for a Brazilian, Mexican or Chilean solution. He concludes: "The problem is that Brazil has few or no intellectuals who seek to formulate alternative policies. There may be some, the "Brazilian" may allow me to contradict him. The fact is that they have no means of reflecting their proposals in the world or globalized media, in their own "developing" world and especially in the world that has the systems in its hands. They will be able to conquer this space, through hard and persistent work, with the growth of the mass of consciousness, and if there is time before the break."

assistance, on which the government has concentrated its action, withdrawing from other areas, left to the fluctuation - or fury - of the market. One can imagine what has happened, or what is happening to the least competitive - the weakest, including Brazil, left at the mercy of the strongest - the masters of the market, the suction pumps - and also bombs that threaten the world - some of them.

To this market liberalism, leaving the presence of the state limited to promoting social policies, and, of course, ensuring the security of the system, or global control, neoliberalism began to dominate.

With the neo-liberal proposal, conservative forces imagined securing the future of capitalism by maintaining the absolute freedom of the market and the regime of competition and compensating the exclusion of the peripheries with the said social, or welfare policies. Eventually, they also offered alms to countries, forgiving their debts in exchange for their submission and the opening of markets, in an unlimited way, creating the new colonialism.

If the results of such a theory were not contradicted by practice, the offence to ethics and human dignity would become obvious - state welfare taking the place of people's right to work, to income, to participation - to freedom and dignity. On the other hand, in this way, the submission of States is also promoted - States excluded because, for them, at least on the surface, there is no way out. In reality, it must be considered that, if the developed countries have sufficient resources to maintain their assistance programs, the security of the excluded does not exist, precisely because they are required to guarantee resources through the "primary surplus", a beautiful expression created to ensure system profits, even if it is at the expense of exclusion - unemployment, economic stagnation, as if there were no other alternative paths, or as if they were not possible.

Instead of allowing for human development, participation and access, we therefore favour assistance, the donation of food, zero hunger, whatever the name given to the alms card granted, instead of guaranteeing each person the right to work, occupation and income, the only instrument for the promotion of man and his dignity, or his participation in society.

In the wake of this error, marketing systems act, marketing alms, despite the ethical precept: **"let your left hand ignore the alms your right hand gives"**.

I'll digress for a personal statement:

At one point, I imagined raising awareness of the process, suggesting that marketing regarding the distribution of food baskets - I believe it was 600,000 baskets, just over a decade ago, now the goal is to distribute several million baskets because the number of excluded people has increased by the millions, turned into clients of federal, state, municipal programs, well... I imagined raising awareness of the process by suggesting that institutional (government) marketing materials begin as follows:

"The government, once again, apologizes to the Brazilian nation, because, having failed to provide work, income and dignity, or citizenship to a significant part of the population, it is obliged to give alms, once again, to at least guarantee its survival".

I asked the marketing department what it wanted to prove with its figures, that the increase in the welfare policy or exclusion? Or was he simply trying to induce society to support the government at the expense of the essential truth?

The marketers must not even have understood the question.

It is an illusion to think that this fact could sensitize the masters of the systems. I was mistaken. The proposal only outraged them, not for the fact denounced, but for the transparency, where the impact of the truth had to be hidden.

Of course, marketing, which the truth generally disturbs, found the proposal surrealistic, unmarketable. And in that world, I felt like an ET.

I return to the **Third Millennium Revolution**:

In the left-most current, but in the same lineage "reformist" of liberalism from the same point of view of the free market and the maintenance of its presuppositions, is the proposal called the Third Way, which at present (2000) has, in the same countries as its biggest exponents, the British Labour Prime Minister Tony Blair and the American President Bill Clinton. There are no essential differences in the root of the proposals of neo-liberalism and the Third Way, except in the deepening of the responsibility of the State, in the elimination of poverty and in the development of so-called social policies. The proposal of the Third Way goes beyond the internal limits, to also advocate greater responsibility on the part of the rich countries for the eradication of poverty in the Third World, the promotion of aid policies. By way of example, I cite the cancellation of the debts of the poorest or most indebted countries.

It is also interesting to note that these theses, and in this respect the Third Way, which proposes them, a daughter of neo-liberalism, are close to the socialist theses presented in particular by the French socialists, through Prime Minister Lionel Jospin, to the European Union, also in the context of the entry into the new millennium.

However, no one is proposing to change the model, which is at the root of exclusion, which is at the root of poverty.

The **Third Millennium Revolution** continues:

Apparently, they propose small steps, socialism or social democracy, or even neo-liberalism, in the direction of humanization. Only apparently in the direction of humanization, because the proposals, if the conception and mechanisms do not change, will only lead to the continuation of the model or the quest for the survival of the system. This is how the walls of Jericho are built.

To this end, produced during the last 50 years of the last century, at the top of the process, or by the beneficiaries of the systems, the concepts and strategies have not been successful, in line with the reversal of the concentration-exclusion process. On the contrary, concentration and exclusion continue to increase, and now that the Second World - the socialist world - has been defeated, wealth and power are growing and accumulating in the First World, the world of market systems, where in the growing absence of competitors, the threat of world totalitarianism is growing in volume, strengthening the strongest and, among them, the strongest, the new axis of dominant power is being formed. This new axis is driven to its extremes by the provocative strategies of US President George W. Bush, assisted by his satellites.

- Tony Blair in England and Berlusconi in Italy in the foreground, and various other satellites. So we are repeating, with a slight change in partners, the alliance or axis of those who in the forties of the last century tried to dominate the world.

Answers from the desperate.

It is necessary to add a comment on the other side, the side of those who imagine promoting change through alternative strategies: terror, or violence - the violence of the excluded, the desperate or fanaticism in its less sophisticated forms than that of the fundamentalism of the masters of the market, or of global systems.

On this side, of those who propose radical changes, and who also have little perception of the process, crushed by revolt and urgency, the persistence of concepts from the past is revealed above all in the method. In sectors on this side, they claim to promote change at all costs, even if they explode the process, believing, moreover, that only the explosion of the process will bring about change. Among these, violence as a method prevails over the concrete proposal of solutions. Without really knowing where they are going and how they are going to get there, they promote terrorism, guerrilla warfare, kidnappings, confrontation against institutions against people, inspired by all reasons, or none, giving body and position to a new nihilism.

We can also classify in this category, the so-called leftists, the fundamentalists of all faiths, which makes them so similar to the right, concepts, moreover, whether they are left- or right-wing, so empty of content and results, in this post-technological era, a bold, clear and competent step forward - synthesis, not the eternal exchange from right to left and from left to right, i.e. from thesis to antithesis, and from antithesis to thesis, without reaching any synthesis, to use the dialectical concept of history. It is in this line of reasoning that we should ask ourselves:

What changes have the left made in favour of peace, security or the participation of the individual, that is, the humanization of society, or the progress of civilization, where they have taken power, whether in the Soviet Union and its satellites, Cuba, or in China or in the poor countries of Africa? What has been gained from the long dictatorships, during which generations lost their freedom, so that, in the end, everything returns to what it was at the beginning, as happened in the Second World? Or what structural changes have been made in the capitalist countries where the so-called socialist democracies have taken power, as has happened in France, or in Sweden, for example, where "neo-socialism" is in power, or in the African regimes, where the so-called liberalization movements have only ensured that poverty is compounded by violence? Or what changes have fundamentalists in the Arab or Muslim world produced in their theocratic regimes, taking the place of the petrodollar plutocracy, or simply also supported by them?

As we can see, on the one hand, the inefficiency of the left, on the other hand, the resurgence of the right, in their capacity to concentrate and exclude - this is the only result of the "neo" in its various forms, prolonging and reinforcing imbalances, insecurity and the threat of global breakdown.

And isn't it true that the world, restless and worried, is watching?

In reality, what he is looking at could be compared to a surrealist dance where the indomitable forces of the capitalist countries - or of the right, imagine radically changing the model, pushing it towards socialism, while in the socialist countries, or on the left, in the same illusion, disillusioned by socialism, return to the capitalist model. In this surrealist dance, there are only steps to the side, instead of a step forward. In this way the process is immobilized. In the dialectical conception of history, I repeat, one continually returns from the thesis to the antithesis, and from the antithesis to the thesis, instead of promoting synthesis, capable of avoiding disturbances and ensuring the natural course of the history of civilization, or of human evolution.

The formation of regional blocs.

To conclude this brief analysis of the survival strategies promoted by those who imagine maintaining the current model indefinitely, the tendency to form regional blocs deserves to be considered, with a view to increasing the competitive capacities of each one and, by improving their competitiveness, eliminating the competitor.

Since this strategy is designed on the assumption of eliminating the competitor; or by concentrating, excluding the competitor, it does not change the current model in any way. It only exacerbates the ability to compete, allowing the process to survive until the last competitor is eliminated. Therefore, as long as the model lasts, there will be no limits to global totalitarianism.

It could have a different meaning, however, the creation of supranational blocs, if they were oriented towards the paths of cooperation among their members and participation on a global scale - globalization in the respect for regional identities; a plurality of cultures; the promotion of deconcentrated and non-exclusive economies. Following this path, the strategy of forming regional blocs could represent a step towards the post-technological society.

If this is not the case, however, the strategy for forming regional blocs will be just one more instrument to delay the break-up. And by delaying it, it will only make it greater, when it takes place, or if it takes place, by the growth of imbalances resulting from the postponement of its outcome.

Once the alternative is defined, the question is:

Why would it be impossible to take a step forward, or why should man always have to go back to the past, denying himself the process of evolution through complementarity, attraction, cooperation and participation, going against the nature of this process, composing the wrong note in the symphony of nature? Would it be its destiny to destroy itself, being endowed with conscience and the conditions for the exercise of freedom?

In reality, it is the very nature of nature and its processes that lead to cooperation rather than competition; to participation rather than exclusion; to complexity and pluralism rather than monopolies; to harmony and balance rather than imbalance and conflict; to peace, cooperation, solidarity and love rather than terror, war, concentration and exclusion.

To visualize, finally, the imbalances or disharmony produced by the order of concentration, the map drawn up by an intelligent report by the magazine Carta Capital in 1996 - based on the JP Morgan report - shows what the geopolitics of the world would be like if countries were divided according to the size of their wealth instead of that of their territory - today the distortion would be much greater. The map shows how half of the countries would simply disappear from the world as a continent - Africa would be reduced to a little more than a point, and South America a little more, at the expense of the monstrous growth of other countries.

The same distortion would surely occur if the link was made between wealth and population, wealth and natural resources, and other indicators that show the size of the distortions and the path of global imbalances.

In nature, every monstrous organism is doomed to die; and the unbalanced structure is doomed to collapse. Sometimes the organism is doomed to produce many evils, or to suffer much pain before death; and the structure too is doomed to generate much uncertainty before it collapses. Would the social organization be different from the nature or structure of the house of men?

Map No. 01 - The Political Map of the World, drawn according to the level of concentration of wealth and in detail, the actual drawing.

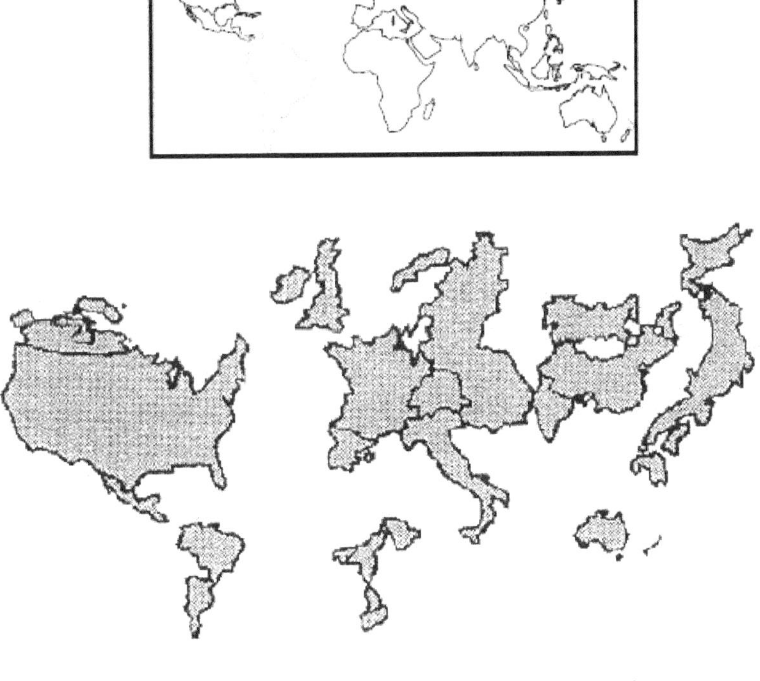

4.   THE THREAT OF GLOBAL TOTALITARIANISM.

As long as resistance to change prevails, alongside the imbalance in society and the threat of the destruction of the planet, it will pose a greater threat to humanity: the establishment of a new form of totalitarianism, different from all known forms in history, revolving around civilization.

Different from all forms of totalitarianism that have been realized or known, because the new totalitarianism is turning into a world dictatorship and because it is settling in a hidden way, behind systems that are apparently modern and efficient, but which condition the way people act and think, unifying what should be made complex and multiple, as a presupposition of the existence of freedom and as a direction for the evolution of man and the universe, according to what has been analyzed previously.

This new form of totalitarianism exercised by systems and hidden behind them affects individuals, groups and all social structures, as well as countries and nations.

On the other hand, hidden totalitarianism does not make it clear who the dictators - the masters of the systems - are. Previously, dictators had unmistakable outlines, names, identities or moustaches that identified them and allowed them to be abhorred in front of society, or in front of history.

Today, even though they may have their representatives, whether it is the President of the United States or his cronies, or the leaders of the banana republics, they are manipulated by diffuse, almost virtual power, or global interests, which produces technology and also allows it to be constituted.

As far as countries are concerned, the new totalitarianism is being exercised with contempt for national sovereignties, as in the past, or as has happened recently in Iraq, Iran, which can be cited as an example, or wherever general interests can be confronted in real or fictitious ways.

However, the new totalitarianism also has subtler and sophisticated forms of intervention, through diplomatic pressure or the armed threat of nuclear and electronic weapons of all kinds and their untouchable arsenals, which can be neither monitored nor controlled.

In reality, according to the masters of the systems, the non-dissemination of the destruction devices - their monitoring and dismantling - is a necessary principle, but only applicable to others - to the weakest.

For themselves, it is only permissible to dismantle the obsolete arsenal, while by the strategy of war, old arsenals are dismantled and new ones are tested, fired at cities and people in the name of civilization, democracy and freedom - thus prostituting themselves.

In the same way, national sovereignties will be suppressed, and supranational bodies will also end up being threatened, subjected to global totalitarianism, which is undoubtedly the greatest achievement of this civilizational transition.

The diversity of cultures is eliminated through the means of communication supported by the marketing of products, processes and everything that we want to sell in the world - not just goods but ideas, fashions, gestures, habits and customs. Art, ethics, or the lack of them, are introduced, suffocating and eliminating local cultures in equal measure.

Pluralism, creativity, freedom is therefore killed, and, what is more serious, they are killed subliminally, by appeasing consciences - the opposite path of the growth of the mass of consciousness.

People do not perceive the process they are going through.

The diversity of philosophies and thought are eliminated.

Already in the 1920s of the last century, the Portuguese poet Fernando Pessoa quoted the pain of thinking in several of his poems. It hurts all the more today because the media, the systems think for everyone and have the means to propagate what they think on a global scale, and this with the power of the technology they possess.

We must return to Orwell and record the loss of individuality, stolen by the systems, controlled and formatted by them.

The space for people to exercise their own skills diminishes unless they fit into the systems and their binary programs.

Meanwhile, the electronic eye monitors everyone's privacy at work, in the street, in the shelter of the home, finally, within the limits of what the remnants of ethics, or the sensitivity of institutions, in the face of legal systems out of step, wish to establish.

In this way, just as we limit the sovereignty of nations, presupposing their freedom (at the time of free homelands!), we limit or eliminate the diversity of cultures, the pluralism of ideas, individual freedoms.

This process is a real threat and is not fiction. It may not reach the extremes, if the process is reversed, and technology and its use, inspired by ethics and law, oriented towards pluralism, participation and human solidarity, as it could be, and should be, and the survival of civilization will increasingly require that it be.

Otherwise, totalitarianism will inexorably lead the process to rupture, because the totalitarian model goes against the nature of man and the universe, or its evolutionary process.

Meanwhile, the men will continue to transform their houses into bunkers or fortresses, surrounded by bars, with guards and dogs to defend themselves. The heads of state, the masters of the systems, in particular, will move around in their war operations, for their conciliations of power, hijacked by planes, tanks, soldiers in the streets, ships displaced in the seas - this too is not fiction - but to protect themselves from what? After all, aren't they - or do they not consider themselves to be - the representatives of the earth, or of civilization? Or would they be aliens displaced in time and space, trying to conquer the earth, or to maintain its rules of the game on it? Sometimes it seems so, because their actions ignore mankind.

The poor and the excluded are resigned, worried or revolted, with nothing to lose but life, but they know that they cannot defend it from death by disease, hunger, malnutrition, or repressive fire, or by a rocket or warhead accidentally diverted from its course, or electronically driven by those who promote war. They will eventually be ready for anything, because life, once freedom and dignity have been taken away, no longer contains or is no longer a value.

Has man reached the third millennium, perhaps after tens of millennia of history, to build a society of totalitarianism, fear or terror?

Would he have developed the technology for his own insecurity and death instead of life?

No, certainly not, because nature is not suicidal. But for that, we must build alternative paths. These paths exist, are possible and sustainable, and we must begin to travel them or to build them (it is by moving forward that we build paths[22]) before it is too late, and the price to be paid for arriving at the new civilization, the post-technological society, is, therefore, intolerable.

---

[22]Pablo Neruda

PART III

THE POST-TECHNOLOGY SOCIETY:

1. INTRODUCTORY REMARKS.

1.1 THE CHALLENGE OF CHANGE.

Realizing the nature of the process and its distortion is important. But the construction of the alternative future is even more important, especially when one is aware that this construction is possible. To do this, we must begin by identifying the essential, or strategic, changes that are appropriate to promote the new civilizational order or new forms of coexistence and human relations between people and between peoples and nations, in this era transformed by technology. Will man be able to take the step necessary for this change, in the same dimension, or scope determined by his cry - technology? Or will the fate of the absurd be that of the human species, repeating the role of the sorcerer's apprentice and ending up being a victim of its own creation?

Human nature and the mass of consciousness.

The most common objection to the possibility of building a humanized society, or promoting the necessary revolution of the third millennium, making possible the society of the post-technological era, based on new values and new ethical foundations, is that its viability would require an ideal, perfect, or almost perfect man. It is said that such a man does not exist. His history would prove it, as well as his own process of competition and concentration - as it happens, and how it produces its consequences, too.

There is some truth in the objection, but it contains an enormous misunderstanding of the essential nature of man and the evolutionary process inherent in him, a subject which is dealt with in the first part of this book.

In this sense, we must consider that we are not proposing to build a humanized society for the man of the past, but for the man in the process of evolution, the man of the present moment, who has been able to create technology and who is therefore accelerating - or urgently needs to accelerate - his own process of transformation and development.

It is not rational that, having accelerated the process of transforming things, he remains in a static conception of his own history, as if the history of humanity were an aberration of nature. And there lies the misunderstanding.

What little truth there is in the argument is that the perfect man does not exist, indeed, at least at this stage, and at no other, as long as the human condition continues. This is due to his concrete nature.

There is, however, man in the process of evolution, and it is on this conception that the viability of the proposal is based. Therefore, the error is to deny that man, being part of all nature, carries within him, like all nature to which he belongs, the seed, or the essential impulse to evolve - they improve, physically, biologically, socially and ethically. As well as psychologically and spiritually.

It is not true, therefore, to say that the human species is not evolving. If some men find it difficult to evolve, focusing on the past of their origin, the primacy of instinct over consciousness, from the time when they were subject to the forces of nature and therefore needed to compete and impose themselves in order to survive. The fact is that, despite some, human beings as individuals and as a species have so far made great strides in the line of their evolution.

Man no longer lives in caves, untidy, dirty and with an animal's mouth in his hand, to defend or attack, although some still stubbornly wear the mouth - or its equivalent - it is true.

But man is evolving, and a minimum of perception and analysis of history, where reality and the processes that shape the world, shows a growing number of human beings as well as institutions, countries and nations are transforming, reaching new stages of consciousness, in search of new stages of civilization. These new stages are already no longer dictated by the need to survive, but by the perception of the meaning of things, by the way in which technology can be used and the new dimensions it offers to human beings, i.e. by consciousness. The course of this development is moving more and more in the direction of rejecting arrogance and arrogant, excessive ambition or the need for competition, concentration, accumulation and self-assertion, at the risk of promoting exclusion, imbalances and the threat of rupture or destruction of the human process.

On the other hand, concepts, practices and awareness of the new human dimensions are developing in the world: **fraternity, cooperation, the right to participation and the effective and universal exercise of freedom; awareness and practice of human rights, the exercise and feelings of solidarity; the aspiration to justice and peace.**

It is these new values which, day by day, are increasingly becoming the universal conscience, the requirement and condition for the continuity of the civilizational process and the basis for the organization of the post-technological era and the survival of the human species, given the dimensions of their own technology. It is this mass of consciousness that will make, through these values and foundations, the new civilization. The mass of consciousness, the fruit of human evolution itself, uses to its advantage the technology that globalizes everything, including consciousness and not only systems, and will continue, sheltered from other globalized things, to impose itself at the heart of history, to make history, in spite of those who deny the process, out of convenience, interest or fear of the necessary changes. While these resist, technology itself, placed at the service of the mass of consciousness, will continue to contribute to the awakening of new consciousness even in the remotest corners of the world, and this process of universal growth of consciousness - the other side of globalization - will be a great engine of the transformation of civilization.

The moment of mutation.

The meaning of history is therefore irreversible and universal, and the universal growth of the mass of consciousness, mentioned in the evolutionary and technological imperative, is the most obvious proof that this leap in the evolutionary process, or this moment of civilizational mutation, is beginning to occur, also in man. Why should it only happen with technology, science, or things, excluding man, the own universal consciousness from the whole process?

If the process of evolution is, essentially, a process of complexification to be continually ordered, so that it does not turn into chaos - disaggregation and death, is it acceptable that consciousness - the instrument of ordered complexity, should itself be eliminated from the process?

In fact, the increasing complexity of the process at an ever-increasing pace, now driven by the technological leap, makes the process of the continuous organization of society urgent and provoking, because only an evolved consciousness, by inserting new foundations and values into the structures and new forms of human relationships, will prevent the process from becoming chaotic, and becoming self-destructive. It is obvious that this process affects all social institutions and requires, as a presupposition, a continuous repositioning of each individual, so that each can insert himself into reality - permanently modified and mutating, an extension of himself, of man, as Ortega y Gasset teaches.

Some researchers in the field of physiology and genetics are beginning to establish a relationship between the evolution of the human species and the changes that would take place in cell structure and the DNA chain, in parallel with transformations in the world of technology. There are those who go further, concluding that these changes may represent a critical moment in the mutation of the human species in that process. Such a hypothesis would make sense if it produced in the human species the same leap that took place in the world of technology - preparing man to live in the post-technological era. If confirmed, the hypothesis amplifies the theses of this book, uniting the change in the human race with the change in technology of civilization with the sense of the evolution of the human species itself, but it does not seem that this leap of mutation is a necessary presupposition for this change, although it broadens its meaning.

Whatever form it takes, the fact is that the moment of change exists and we are living it, despite those who do not perceive it, or imagine that they can prevent it from happening. It is not likely that the process will allow them to continue to order the world as if nothing were happening, trying to prevent the course of history, or of human evolution, until somehow the rupture takes place. History will undoubtedly survive, they won't.

The challenge and its scope.

This perspective is the challenge for all those who feel included in the process as members of the human species, and builders of their own history, their environment, or humanity, whatever:

- the challenge of those who believe, those who make science, those who care about the human process, about individuals and institutions, about universities by their specificity as centres of knowledge production and innovation and by their mission, therefore, to create synthesis, amidst so many theses and antitheses, stratified and dangerously contradictory. They must, in particular, research or conceive the theory of the new organization of society, after the technological leap - which would make social organization appropriate to the post-technological reality. The necessary theory, as a synthesis, will have to cover all the elements that make up society - economy, politics, law, ethics, new rules, finally, for the organization and sustainable coexistence of man in the globalized and technological world: it will also have to be inserted in his environment, which is also affected by technology. This means that it will have to allow respect and preservation, sustainable use and coexistence with nature; diversity of cultures, races; peaceful coexistence of peoples and countries, cooperation and solidarity by promoting pluralism, participation and sustainability in this complex, dynamic and interdependent world. The challenge of those who think the world and want to build it as a humanized world;

-       The challenge of communicators, those who feed the global computer and information networks, those who dominate the press and the communication media, and those who have these instruments and their immense powers of persuasion, training and consciousness-shaping. The latter, if they misuse the media, have the power to put men's consciousness to sleep, acting against the growth of universal consciousness, (the mass of consciousness); instead of contributing to the awakening of consciousness and the acceleration of change;

-       The challenge for intellectuals, to assume the ability and courage to break the inertia, the convenience, the compromise with the past, without hatred and prejudice, but with the competence to define horizons, to identify and order the new values and to develop the tools for each segment of the process and the global instruments capable of organizing the post-technological society in its different components, with objectivity and scientific spirit, focused on man and nature, of which man is a part, without fear of innovating in ideas and proposals and free from interests and stereotypes ;

-       The challenge of the churches and religions in general, with their strength to move wills and give rise to revolts, fears or hopes, when they discover that the awakening of consciences is necessary, but not sufficient. It is necessary to point out paths and bring hope to men, but it is also necessary to insert oneself in reality or in the effort to inspire the foundations, forms and instruments, capable of producing the necessary solutions and supporting them;

- the challenge to the leaders of nations and peoples and to all those who command the main segments that constitute social power, so that, attentive and receptive to the process, they are open to innovative thinking and to accepting innovation, far from the same prejudices, their defense and consolidated interests, or because of the convenience of repeating the past, because it is in their hands that the strength to hasten change as much as the capacity to oppose it resides.

In any case, those who oppose change must be aware that, however great their power, they do not possess the power to stop history, or the directions, or the vocation of nature, even though some may think they do, repeating the mistake that so many others in the past have already made.

They'll come to the same end, because no one will remember the story.

The proposal of a change of civilization and the presuppositions and instruments capable of making it viable, therefore, has nothing to do with illuminism, or the voluntarism of the past, or with the simple moralism of the present. Rather, it has to do with the continuation of the process and the necessary advent of a new level of evolution, or with the survival of the human species and its ability to overcome the obstacles that arise in the midst of this process. Indeed, it was the pioneer of the perception of the evolutionary process, Charles Darwin, who said that in the process it will not be the strongest or the most intelligent who will survive, but "those who have a greater capacity to adapt to change", since the ability to adapt to change is a sign of intelligence in man.

This step is possible and inevitable. If it is not given in response to these challenges, through the competence and creativity and the capacity for innovation and evolution of the human species, it will eventually come about through the imperative of history, that is, through the imposition of nature, in reaction to the extremes of imbalance and tension, to which the process could be led. In this case, there will inevitably be an explosion or rupture, as occurs in nature when imbalances or tensions have not been eliminated in time. It will take place, and it does not matter in what dimension or form, but it will surely happen.

1.2   THE SIGNS OF HOPE.

The mistake of those who resist.

In contrast to the essential principles, related to the nature of the evolutionary path of the human species and its organization, some continue -- those who understand the human condition the least -- to think, propose and act as if there were no process and everything came down to situational or predominant factors, interests now represented mainly by the economy, the market, profit, or the accumulation of wealth or power, and other myths that have been introduced, or have been introduced into the process, as the fundamental values related to the nature of man and "his circumstances" have been weakened or lost: society, the environment and, in a broader perspective, the planet itself, or the universe, of which man is a part.

In this context, the myths of the past have been replaced by the deification or predominance, or dictatorship of capital in the hands of the State or individuals and groups, depending on the ideology and interests assumed, and by the conviction that the economy and the market - the visible face of materialism, are the only reality, and the only value, at the altar of which everything must be sacrificed, including man, or human dignity.

Some men act only this way, inspired by these misconceptions. However, these are a decreasing number, and only on the surface they may seem to be getting stronger and stronger because, in reality, they are the masters of the systems and they will be strong as long as the systems that concentrate and focus support them. But their strength is equivalent to that of the walls of Jericho - or the statue of Bahal, the idol with feet of clay, to cite another example of wisdom, drawn from biblical inspiration. Or the towers of the World Trade Center in New York.

Their weakness is exactly this: they are linked to a process that reality has overtaken and, therefore, they will only be strong as long as the mass of consciousness does not take precedence - the cry of the Hebrews around the walls, with which they protect themselves, or as long as they do not realize that their feet are in clay. Without this perception, they move like the assassins condemned by the law of the ancient Egyptians, devoured by vultures in the desert, tied to the corpses of their own victims.

Change is therefore inevitable.

History shows that change has always, or almost always, taken place against or at the margin of those who dominated the systems. This was the case with the Romans in relation to the "barbarian peoples", with the feudal nobility in relation to the bourgeoisie. It can be so now with the bourgeoisie in power - through the new barbarians - the excluded from the systems, whether peasants, workers, landless, unemployed people – the billions of the excluded; or whether it is the Latinos, Asians, Arabs or Africans; or whether it is also those excluded from power, culture, freedom or dignity, the new barbarians or the new bourgeoisie, who will overthrow the ruling empires. How? That is not the point.

The necessary coherence of the process.

The same process of growth of those excluded from the systems is now being repeated through the mass consciousness. However, the mass of consciousness is also growing and increasingly includes larger and larger sections of the societies of those who dominate the systems, or who support the model. These, acting as the leaven in the systems - and part of the mass of consciousness, will help to precipitate change. Thus, the mass of consciousness is not limited to places, classes or nations, but is an expression of human nature itself. In this perspective, the mass of consciousness also develops in central countries - in concentrated and concentrating systems; it grows among intellectuals and communicators; it develops among business and political leaders ; but more and more, above all, among the young, the young generations who, instinctively (the survival instinct), have realized the unsustainability and dehumanization of the process that uses technology in favour of exclusion, violence and war, when it could be used for mankind - participation, peace, solidarity and love.

It is the growth of this mass of consciousness that brings hope that change will occur, and it is through this growth that the paths of hope are opened. Those who do not realize this process, those who oppose it, those who are incapable of ordering hope, have lost the vision of history, and if they do not deviate, they will end up being left out of the process. Saying when and at what cost this will happen belongs to fiction or prophecy and it is not the purpose of this book to detail it. But it would be regrettable if history were to repeat itself as it did in the past - the rupture, because now, because of the dimension of technology and its consequences, and above all because of the magnitude of the imbalances, the rupture can occur on a global scale and therefore much more seriously for man, for humanity and for the planet, man's common home and habitat.

Such analyses may seem to be mere moral concepts. In reality, they are also moral concepts. However, I prefer these concepts to be, and they should be, characterized as ethical concepts because they are essential, not subject to time, culture, conditions or prejudices.

Ethical concepts are an essential part of reality, of the nature of things. Not to consider them is to disfigure reality and, consequently, to start from analyses, conclusions and models that are disfigured, reductionist or unbalanced, and therefore unsustainable. Above all, it should be noted that, being essential, ethical concepts are a source of inspiration and operational tools, making reality and nature coherent. This is how the process becomes sustainable.

This is possible - this coherence between ethics, or the expression of nature, and the instruments of social organization. It is the path of change, or it is the path that will make concrete the hope that will lead the human species to a new civilization, the civilization of the post-technological era, with which the third millennium begins.

1.3   A NEW MEANING FOR MAN.

It may not be appropriate to speak of a new meaning for man, because, in reality, man's sense of self is a constant in his history, despite the deviations that may have occurred along the way. It would be best to speak, therefore, of man's affirmation or fidelity to his own nature.

Process deviations.

Deviations from this process of fidelity to nature can indeed occur and have occurred in history. Within certain limits, these deviations are absorbed by the process, as a consequence of the complexity of the process itself and the limitations and imperfections of human nature.

At this stage, however, and because of the dimensions of the technology, the gaps threaten to go beyond these limits. What is happening is that, in addition to certain errors exacerbated by the power of technology and its use, there is the threat of the loss of the primacy of values inherent in human nature and its dimension, in favour of other values of a lower order, such as economic values, interests of all kinds that often clash with nature. It is this sum that threatens the sustainability of the process.

Among these misconceptions, we can highlight, and it therefore deserves special analysis, the system that produces, concentrates and maintains wealth, profit and the market as determinants of human activity, social organization and its relations, above all values or any ethico-legal criteria required by the evolution of civilization. The aim is not, with this statement, to contest the legitimacy of profit, or of the market, reduced to their proper dimension and meaning, or their necessity as factors that make the economy viable, and therefore important factors for the functioning of society. But there is a big difference between admitting the importance of specific factors and the absence of limits to the intervention of these factors, allocating them all spaces so that they are transformed into an objective, for which other values are sacrificed, perhaps, or surely, as much or more essential than them. This attitude of exclusion constitutes a reductionism whose consequences restructure the social organization, preventing harmony, balance and therefore the sustainability of the process.

In reality, contrary to what is claimed, the economy is not an equation. The equation is society. There is no economic equation. The economy is a term in the equation, which is society, and it is a serious mistake to try to organize the term at the cost of disorganizing the equation, as is happening in the current model.

The primacy of profit - of the term over the equation, of the concentration of wealth and of speculation as an instrument to produce it - is exercised without taking into account its consequences, namely social imbalance and the destruction of human values, which are essential for the existence of an organization whose sustainability is linked to the progress of civilization, and which make it appropriate at every moment.

The stage of civilization we have reached, and its complexity, the strength and dimension of technology, and the growing demands of mass consciousness, do not allow deviations of the dimension of those who threaten the process to continue to prevail, but require the creation of conditions capable of maintaining its balance and correcting the deviations.

A new concept of profit and quality of life.

Therefore, the present moment requires a radical change of concepts, starting with the concept of profit, transformed from the simple factor that it is a simple factor into an absolute and principal instrument and objective of human organization and actions, as it is conceived and practiced. It is not enough, however, to put profit back in its rightful place - from the simple instrument that it is, to the supreme aim of organization and human relations.

This set of goods, in which everyone has the natural right to participate, covers the material, cultural and spiritual goods that make up a society and are part of the human dimension: **material goods, as a prerequisite; harmony and balance of social organization that engender security; access and tolerance that engender peace and the coexistence, cooperation and support that generates love.**

In the context of the ease of producing wealth in the virtual economy, or of producing goods in the real economy, the very notion of profit as a financial result becomes a concept that must be relativized by the prevalence of the promotion of values expressed by the mass of consciousness, already characterized. In this context, it must be borne in mind that the product, as a consumption of material goods, is inelastic, and can therefore easily saturate demands with the capacity of technology to produce them. Only goods related to consciousness-spirituality in the broadest sense of the term-can grow indefinitely. Yet it is these, and not these, that give meaning to human evolution.

It is not rational, in fact, to order or to imagine that one can order the post-technological society only by factors of a financial or virtual nature, or by the accumulation of material goods, wealth or power, limited and limiting factors, which are also capable of inserting into the process unlimited imbalances, creating insecurity and unsustainability. It is this gap in the process that we are experiencing.

It is more rational to build society according to the nature of the processes, to impose limits on the factors capable of producing imbalances and to promote alternative factors capable of ensuring that harmony takes precedence over imbalance, that well-being and better living conditions, or the continuous growth of quality of life in the sense of human fulfilment - happiness? - take precedence over profit, the market, goods - this is the meaning of growth, or the complexity of being organized.

This alternative vision does not exclude profit - it would be preferable to speak of the result of human activities - as an instrument to make the increased production of goods viable, to make the available goods more abundant and, consequently, to facilitate access, participation and greater inclusion, instead of continuing to produce imbalances and exclusion.

This alternative notion of profit may seem like a negation of crystallized concepts, or a revolution of stratified concepts and practices, on which economic science is based. But technology has also been a revolution, overcoming traditional and stratified practices, which might seem to its contemporaries to be heresy, dream or fiction. However, technology is there to condition the process, and to demand that balance be restored, that human factors be present, and that the process of civilization be continued in a sustainable manner.

It is in this context and according to this conception, that on profit, competition and concentration, universal aspirations, or the quest, for quality of life and human fulfilment gain meaning, making the mass of consciousness a criterion and an instrument of change, capable of inspiring new rules of organization and civilized coexistence .... Is it by chance that too much is demanded of human rationality to be able to organize society and its environment - the environment around it - according to human aspirations, the state of progress of the evolutionary process and the conditions brought about by the technological revolution?

Why should the opposition between sentiment, the same human aspirations, or man's own nature, and the possibilities of technology be maintained and cultivated in the quest to build a social, political, ethical and economic organization that is human and therefore sustainable? 4

An alternative criterion of balance sheet, or social wealth.

The answer to this question requires the development of instruments capable of accounting for the balance of well-being, satisfaction or quality of life or the conditions for human fulfilment (- human happiness?) as essential components of the stage of development or evolution of a society - the actual balance of their wealth.

These concepts will be difficult to understand or accept per se, in its assumptions and consequences, by those who are conditioned by the traditional concepts of profit, competition, concentration, the market as the raison d'être, cause and effect of human actions and their reactions. The same difficulty will arise for those who do not believe in the global capacity to produce enough, or abundant, goods to meet the global demands of the world's population.

However, it must be considered that even what is produced today, with an effort to rationalize production, even without the sophisticated use of all that technology allows to be produced, could allow adequate participation by all in the goods produced. The world GDP divided by the population of the planet, would result in an average income of more than 5000 dollars per capita. So there is no shortage of goods. There is a lack of mechanisms to produce them properly and to promote their access in a participatory way to the entire human population, restoring the balance.

To generate the appropriate mechanisms to enable this participation, the initial posture will be to replace, or at least improve, the existing concepts on which economic analysis and financial balance sheets are based - or the profit that drives the economy and the world - with more complex and organized concepts, rather than the simplistic, merely quantitative or reductionist concepts that are the current ones.

Studies already exist on alternatives whose lineage would be that the accounting or wealth to be accounted for, instead of being merely financial, would include or be based mainly on social indicators, committed, therefore, to people, in the expression of the natural resources, and finally in goods capable of satisfying people and their coexistence, giving meaning and value to their lives, and not only to money. This new approach to accounting is still vague, or insufficient to express the real dimension of the components of this new consciousness that is being formed in the world. But this must be the way.

The Human Development Index (HDI), developed by the United Nations, which goes beyond simple criteria of profit or income as indicators of a society's reality, is a first step. This year in Brazil, in partnership with UNDP, a UN body, a report on the "better living conditions for young people". That's a step forward. The social balance sheets of companies and institutions should also be included as an important step in the same direction.

But we have to go much further.

These balance sheets must be given an economic content. They must be expressed as an economic value of society and not as parallel or "compensatory" analyses of the registers of the economy.

A little more than a simple provocation, an assessment of quality of life, or social or human conditions, transformed into economic value, could be formulated, for example, as a very simple equation of the type: $A + B + C + D + E = X$, where:

A - would mean the contribution of certain measures, or of goods produced, to the promotion of well-being and quality of life in society - the frequency or number of measures taken and their results;

B - the stock of awareness, knowledge, culture, appropriate technologies available, how these technologies are distributed among the population, and how and according to what they are used;

C - the availability of natural, human and infrastructure resources;

D - the political (decision-making) will of social movements (political, economic, intellectual, etc.) to use these stocks and availabilities;

E - Inventories and financial results of the economic process;

X - an index representative of the stock of goods and services, satisfaction and quality of life available to promote human inclusion and participation or the well-being, (happiness?) of a society, here representing the result of the equation.

The result of this equation could be a model for negotiations, or trade, or a determining indicator of a country's risk or reliability, or an expression of its ability to own or acquire goods, or to have the conditions necessary for a person or a society to produce its own well-being or ensure its own development - human development, and to interact cooperatively and sustainably with other societies, rather than simply competing, conflicting or necessarily exclusively. Such an exercise would surely identify risks and opportunities better than mere financial balance sheets.

In a way, it is possible to say that this could be the new expression of the "wealth of nations". Alternative formulas along the lines of the proposed example, well developed, more or less sophisticated, more or less operational, could express values, potentialities, conditions or objective situations much more complex and representative than the traditional concept of profit, or financial result, which only considers profit and its reasons as an expression of wealth.

These alternative concepts would be a much more important expression of wealth, of the goods of a society, of the "state" of people's fulfilment, especially when the expression of profit is the result of virtual speculation without any foundation in reality, in the concrete situation of man, his conditions and his living environment - nature and society.

The questions that can't be killed come up again.

Is it really a heresy to look for these indicators, or more complex content, when all nature is increasingly complex? A dream? A revolution? Why can't it be a bit of everything and, above all, a path towards the leap of civilization? By any chance, hasn't this been considered like a dream, a heresy, or a revolution, when someone said that man would be able to fly, to produce human life out of the womb, to travel to the moon, to integrate on a global scale in networks to speak or see each other simultaneously all over the world, to name just a few "heresies" or some of the dreams that made the technological revolution?

In addition to the field of technology, when Pope Paul VI put forward the proposition that development is a process of being more, and not simply of having more, one could not imagine how this could be possible*. However, when the United Nations launched indicators to measure human development instead of using indicators measuring only economic growth - or, what was worse, only financial condition, they also denigrated this proposal, seeing it only as a dream - the product of dreamers, or an ethical or simply moral perspective, with no practical viability. However, in spite of them, these are the steps that are being taken and are leading the way to the new civilisation.

Some will stay on the side of the road.

Concepts develop and become reality.

New concepts, such as some of those already mentioned, are developing and consolidating in various forms, giving rise to clues, or expressions of a reality that is larger, more complex and better adapted to the human dimension and the time of its evolution, than the econometric simplification of the concepts that still order social organization and its relationships. They are taught in universities, dictate the vision of analysts and government policies that create or condition imbalances.

Complexifying, rather than reducing or minimizing analyses or indicators is, however, a requirement of the process of evolution of man and society, and the stage that the post-technology world has reached, history or the human race. At the same time, technology can capture and manage complexity, unlike what is usually done with it - using it to simplify complexity by introducing an erroneous and castrating reductionism of the essential richness of reality, which is found in complexity, pluralism and freedom and not in "simplifying everything and putting it in the system or on the network". The network, like the systems, is exactly what makes it possible to identify and manage complexity, if we consider the human dimension, rather than the easy, dominating and simplistic vision.

Some insist that this perspective would require the development of qualitative indicators. This is true - and this request is a step forward. It must be understood that if the process has been able to produce complexity, the process, and the man with it, must also be able to capture and sustain complexity. Therefore, these indicators will be identified as investment efforts are made by universities, research centers, governments and all those interested in the process of human development. After all, the quantitative indicators, always predominant, and the qualitative indicators already adopted - economic, or social - were not created overnight either, or by magic, or simply by some kind of voluntarism. They are the result of the effort that has now become necessary to develop more complex indicators, with a high qualitative content, and therefore more adapted to the new society.

There will be those who will continue to judge this mission to be an impossible one. For them, for those who are unable to admit or imagine new things, we can also tell them that they are not original.

In the sixteenth or seventeenth century, similarly, those who were fixated on concepts that had ordered the feudal world, were unable to understand the concepts of profit, capital, or the market, as indicators that arrived then in the context of a new and different form of social organization. And the Romans, or going further back, the Greeks, Egyptians, and Babylonians at the height of their power, and at the stage of their civilization, they did not conceive of a world different from the world they dominated. Besides, even before that, cavemen, or tribal man, too ... well, the history is ancient: the beneficiaries of the status, the masters of power, or of knowledge, or the beneficiaries of the systems, or the accommodated, have never understood it, nor have they ever believed in it. That they now understand it, or that they believe it, would require of them more than a revolution...

Finally, on new concepts or new ways of living, and coexisting, there will always be those who find reasons not to accept them, even if those reasons are the reasons of the wolf, the fable of the wolf and the lamb.

Therefore, if, on the one hand, we deepen the concepts and the innovations they generate in line with the construction of a new civilizational order - the mass of consciousness, on the other hand, the resistance to the adoption of measures that lead to sustainability becomes more acute. An example of this is the resistance to signing and accepting the Kyoto Protocol, aimed at controlling and reducing pollution on the planet, or implementing the commitments made at various conferences such as the Earth Summit, the Rio de Janeiro Conference and Rio + 10 Johannesburg, for example, and similar initiatives. These initiatives, although they are concrete proposals - such as the adoption of a tax on the use of natural resources, or the establishment of taxes for the preservation of biodiversity or environmental resources - the diversion of carbon, for example, have little effectiveness. For the time being, and because of resistance, or reasons of the wolf ...

The same resistance focuses on changing trade protectionism, establishing new rules ordering relations of concentration and exclusion, or the unlimited right granted to systems, to step on national sovereignties or individual rights, all according to the prevalence of economic, profit and speculative, albeit virtual, reasons over human rights and dignity.

Examples that line up towards the advent of the inevitable post-technological civilization, or proposals for change towards a humanized civilization, because they diverge with the global interests of those who command the systems, or the beneficiaries of the current order, will always face resistance. However, as history shows, such resistances are very fragile from the perspective of history, despite their strength at the time or during the current situation. Their control, however, will only last until they collapse, like Baal, the idol with feet of clay, from the biblical story, or the towers of the World Trade Center in New York, before the terrified eyes of humanity.

Some may say, finally, that the proposal is too radical. Maybe it is. But it is certainly less radical than the radicalism of technological change - from walking or riding horses, to flying at the speed of sound, or beyond; from sending messages by means of horsemen or horse-drawn carriages, or by smoke signals or banging drums, to sending them at the speed of light; or from conditioning in place and time to participation in global reality, or perhaps virtual reality, or perhaps virtual reality, overcoming one's own conditioning or limitations of space and time. What about penetrating into the intimacy of matter or into the essence of life, manipulating genes and acting on vital processes? Isn't this much more radical than any proposal for social progress? Why should social organization continue as it did in the pre-technological era, the one before the process of innovation took place. that changed the world?

Why should only concepts those of social organization, which includes economics, politics, culture, ethics, and everything else, why should only these concepts remain fixed and immobilized, as if the revolution that has brought reality into line with the demands of technology and where social organization fits in had not been radical?

Why refuse the revolution that remains to be made, - the post-technological civilization, and aggravate, with this refusal, the dysrhythmia or imbalance of the process, which accelerates and makes each day more irreversible the path towards the break, if technology itself were to lead us to the humanized society, realizing the values and aspirations expressed in the mass of consciousness that is formed in a global dimension, coherent with the sense of human nature and their vocation to evolve towards a greater and more continuous perfection, an arrow launched from the Alfa point to reach the Omega point, in the infinite path of history?

1. THE FOUNDATIONS OF THE COMPANY POST-TECHNOLOGY.

1.1 - DEFINITION OF THE FOUNDATIONS.

Ethical relationship of the foundations.

I come back to what was set out in the book **The Third Millennium Revolution,** the second part of which is devoted to the analysis of the foundations proposed for the organization of the new society - the post-technological society. The analysis of the foundations to be followed, however, incorporates the concepts of the "**Third Millennium Revolution**" enriched by the debates and contributions that this book has made possible.

In fact, the ideas in the book have been submitted to dozens of debates in universities, congresses, symposia and other forums, which have only served to validate the proposed foundations. For this reason, I use this part of his text, with some insertions or revisions, because of their validation. In a way, the proposal also expresses the feeling of those thousands of people who have read it, discussed it and, in these debates, have validated it. These people are also part of the mass of consciousness that will make the revolution necessary - the one that remains to be done, after the technological revolution.

Thus, the proposed fundamental principles legitimized as a contribution to the struggle to reverse the course of the process that is moving towards rupture, guiding it in favour of the survival and continuity of human evolution "and its circumstances" - society, nature, the planet, finally, of which man is a part - and an essential part, as consciousness of the Universe, I repeat.

To this end, it is necessary that these foundations become or inspire the operational instruments capable of producing the organization and functioning of society, in all its components, as noted: the economy, culture, politics, social relations and all its components organization and its functioning, overcoming their condition of simple ethical principles, human aspirations, dreams, or simple voluntarist assertions. In any case, it must be remembered that this instrumentalization does not take away the ethical dimension of the proposed foundations, it only makes them operational, establishing coherence between ethics and reality. In this context, the new ethics constitute as much, or more, than individual ethics, a collective ethics of a universal or global nature. Let me give an example: traditional technology did not allow a human being to kill another human being, even if the technology - the means available - made it possible to do so.

Now technology allows us to destroy not only individuals, but nations, economies, cultures. In other words, what used to be only an individual relationship, or a little more, has today become a global ethical condition, because of the global dimension of technology. Therefore, it is not because technology makes it possible to destroy nations, cultures, economies, and populations are decimated by global, or virtual, wars, or by exclusion and its consequences, it is not because technology makes it possible to do so, that these procedures can be ethically or legally acceptable, since ethics, like law, are expressions of the nature of things, or of facts, and technology, or its use, does not change this nature.

It is therefore necessary, in the name of ethics and law, i.e. the nature of things and the process of human evolution, and therefore its survival, that the power of technology be used in favour of cooperation, solidarity and participation, i.e. for mankind, towards the new civilization, the post-technological civilization or the third millennium, rather than being used in the service of concentration and exclusion - that produce, with exclusion, imbalance; or to put at the service of war - which seeks control and which, like exclusion, produces death.

Ethical and practical foundations.

The foundations of the post-technological social order therefore comprise two expressions: one ethical and the other practical or operational.

From an ethical point of view, the fundamental principles proposed to enable post-technological social organization can be summed up as **participation and solidarity**, which are opposed to exclusion and competition, marks and consequences of the organization that is still imposed on society, despite the technological revolution. **Participation and solidarity** sum up the universal aspirations of justice, peace, fraternity and **overcoming concentration without limits**, generating exclusion. **Participation and solidarity** establishes coherence between the aspirations of the prevalence of universal love for people, humanity and nature, thus expressing the essential content of the growing mass of consciousness. As ethical elements of the new society, **participation and solidarity** mean repulsion to prepotency and egocentrism, conflict and war - all of which represent the destructive legacy of mankind and generate imbalances, gaps and unsustainability.

From a practical, or operational point of view, these ethical concepts are allowed, through mechanisms capable of promoting **deconcentrating** in all areas of social structure and relations. The identification, development and use of these concepts must inspire programming, directing investments and organizations of society, transmitting them to people, a condition for access and inclusion. At the same time, the same ethical concepts must inspire the practical mechanism of **cooperation,** which allows a new form of human relationship, participative and supportive, replacing competition, which concentrates and excludes.

In other words: unifying and making ethical and operational points of view coherent, de-concentration fosters participation that promotes pluralism and freedom, in the same way that cooperation fosters solidarity and the growth of human, civilized coexistence, or peace, contributing to the process of building a new, more humane, more amorphous society.

I take the vision proposed in "**The Third Millennium Revolution**"...

1.2 - THE SCOPE AND CONTENT OF DECONCENTRATION AND PARTICIPATION.

Concentration, deconcentration and technology.

The process of concentration, which we have analyzed, with its consequences, has its origin in the concepts produced from the seventeenth century onwards, of capital accumulation as an instrument for increasing wealth creation in the context of the affirmation of the individual and nationality, in the principles of liberalism. These concepts allowed the emergence and growth of industry and other conglomerates, which occupied their spaces within their limits, or limitations imposed by the technology of the time and competed with each other, in their multiplicity, according to those limits. It also gave rise to colonialism, not only as a simple consequence of discoveries, but as an instrument to supply the centers where capitalism was being formed. The possession of technology - starting with the invention of the steam engine - the development of positive science, of things and their administration, which territorial inventions and discoveries, amplifying spaces and providing raw materials, made it possible to apply, consolidated the new social organization around capital - and not man. But man still had a place, because of the limits that technology imposed on concentration.

The investments coming from this system, dictating new rules and procedures, shifted the axis of social organization from the castles of feudal power and distribution in urban areas and the new social organization that was beginning to emerge. In this context, however, the concentration was, because of this limitation of science itself and its application - technology, and producing the first and small technological revolution. The new technological revolution, starting in the twentieth century, however, with the impressive advances in science and its application - the new technology, has imprinted the process of competition and concentration, at an increasing speed, rapidly eliminating, and continuing indefinitely to eliminate competitors, in an increasingly global framework, one after the other. In this process, soon there will not even be competition, if the holders of the new technology, of what it allows to accumulate, continue to occupy all the spaces, concentrating all the wealth and, more and more, all the power, in a process that, in addition to being indefinitely cumulative, will become more and more globalized and absolute.

The proposed deconcentration process will allow the opposite path to be followed. It will use technology to ensure that wealth, power, instruments of communication, culture, knowledge are once again produced and that participation is increasingly broad, multiplying at the base of society, returned to the people, to the multiplicity of groups, regions and nations. In this way, pluralism will grow and, with pluralism, people's freedom and access to the process will grow, i.e. participation will grow. This reversal of the process is possible - because technology, in the same way that it enables or produces concentration, can enable deconcentration and, therefore, access or participation.

It is important to understand that technology is perfectly suited to deconcentrated models, as it allows to identify, capture, organize and manage complexity. All that is needed is for those who possess it - the public authorities and social operators - to use it for this purpose.

This means that technology is not opposed, on the contrary, it is part of complex society and, therefore, of the logic of history - mystics will say: by karma that controls man's destiny; and believers will say : by the providence of God who watches over his creation - whatever the reason, technology has arrived, at this point in the evolutionary process, to enable and order the process of complexification of all things, including man and his circumstances - society and all its system of relationships - and not to deny it, by the misuse that can be made of it - and has been made of it until now. The practice of some people in their management processes, who seek to simplify everything, making everything binary so that they can put everything in the computer, in the system, or in the networks, as they justify, and it has been said, this practice is therefore a mistake.

The development of technology - the use of the computer, or computer systems, however, should lead to the opposite practice, namely, being able to identify or grasp complexity, to order it, and to manage it, because the computer and its systems make it possible to identify and manage complexity, or to live with complexity. Now we have already seen that only complexity produces pluralism, and only pluralism - ordered complexity - allows freedom.

The network society allows for pluralism. But it can also produce the opposite if it is misused.

Thus, deconcentration, which is a process of deverticalization of social organization, by increasing the points or units that make up its base, offers multiple channels or paths of access, or participation in the process, for most elements of the social structure, people, organizations, institutions of all kinds, allowing them to participate in a free and orderly manner, and not only as parts of monolithic systems, imposed without alternatives. The alternative path to monolithic systems, where there is room only for those who conform, according to the number of places and the form established for them to conform, however, is one possible way. All that is needed is for government policies, systems and society to adopt and give precedence to mechanisms leading to deconcentration and cooperation, instead of concentration and exclusion.

Broadening the base, increasing the points, or deconcentrating, as an instrument to facilitate participation, in a free and orderly way, that is, in a way that is consistent with the nature and meaning of its evolutionary process, constitutes the first organizational foundation of the complex post-technological society. The necessary deconcentration must be made possible in the conception, planning and practice of public, or governmental, action, as well as in the demands and requirements of society. It must be sought and made operational in the initiatives of companies, in the formulations of intellectuals and in the institutions of law as a means of enabling a humane, participatory and supportive society. In short: deconcentration is the practical instrument for operationalizing the ethical principle of participation. Or, in other words, **the ethical principle of participation is made possible, becomes operational through deconcentration**, in the same way that, as we shall see later, cooperation constitutes the operational operating principle that enables the ethical principle of solidarity.

Finally, it must also be considered that participation is not a fact that wishes to reach only isolated segments of society, whose structure or sectors, however, may remain concentrated. Essence of this structure, and not just accident, participation must cover all aspects of social organization. Participation that would reach only one segment of the social structure, wealth, for example, but that would leave concentrated power, knowledge, technology, would not restore the balance of society. On the contrary. It could even aggravate imbalances, like any part that develops at the margins, or to the detriment of other parts of the organism.

Presented below with their contents, the analyses set out the current models of deconcentration, in several of these parts, or segments of society: in the economic field; in the demographic and territorial field; in the field of knowledge, technology and culture; in the political field and in the social field. Other segments could also be analyzed, and it should also be considered that the anatomy that is made is only methodological, because all the elements are complementary to each other, and interact forming a single organism - which must be harmonious and balanced to be safe.

Economic deconcentration.

In the economic sphere, deconcentration requires the qualitative, quantitative and instrumental multiplication of production capacity, i.e. of the processes and production units at the base of society. Such multiplication constitutes a strategy and an instrument for developing work and income, allowing the greatest number of people to have access to economic activity and the consequent participation in its results. It has already been discussed in the previous chapter how, in the current system, this access or space for participation is weak and how the process of competition-concentration - making results prevail, perhaps wrongly, over people - produces exclusion, the exclusion of individuals, groups, peoples and entire nations.

It must be borne in mind, because these are often erroneous approaches, that broadening the productive base does not necessarily mean opting for the production of non-sophisticated, coarse, semi-manufactured, semi-industrialised or only craft goods in the least noble sense of the term, which is more noble ... In fact, technological sophistication itself allows more and more sophisticated things to be produced in a distributed way - electronic products and agro-industry, to cite extreme sectors, are examples of this. The issue is much more about design and organization than technological sophistication.

It must also be considered that the capacity for distributed revenue generation is not limited to the products of a physical or material sector. It also covers the production of services, trade and other products and sectors demanded by society. This concept can be overly catalogued, it carries out activities, often informally. Formalizing the activities that exclusion leads to informality, also would be to isolate other malevolent activities to society, many forms of crime and marginality - activities that develop in these areas, often driven by the same process of exclusion.

It must also be considered that the productive capacity that generates distributed income is not limited to the physical, or material, product sector. It also includes the production of services, trade, and other goods or sectors demanded by society. Activities carried out, often informally, can also be categorized under this concept. Formalizing the activities that exclusion leads to informality, one would also isolate other activities that are harmful to society, the different forms of contravention and marginality - activities that grow in these areas that are often pushed back by the same process of exclusion.

It is also necessary to consider that the increase in income is not confused, nor does it come from the simple increase in consumption, which is often highlighted. In a world where one third of humanity is excluded from any form of production or participation in income, or from any productive activity, and so many others survive marginally, the increase in consumption often only deepens the imbalances in favour of concentration, and at the cost of impoverishing the most excluded, seduced by the marketing of the market. These low-income strata, called to join the market, move from consumption to consumerism, first using what little they have, and then what they do not have, making them slaves, literally, of the market. This process also occurs with those countries whose needs, real or fictitious, end up being defined by the interests of those who manipulate systems, markets or speculation, in order to find the best way to invest, even if it is in superfluous and speculation, but with a guarantee of results. Thus, the possible increase in work, or income, through increased consumption, ends up becoming a mechanism for increasing exclusion on the one hand, and contributing to concentration on the other.

Increasing consumption therefore presupposes increasing income, and income generation must be expanded before claiming to increase consumption. I transcribe the analysis of The Third Millennium Revolution (I):

- It is also a mistake to imagine that it is enough to develop employment, even in a concentrated form, or through processes that lead to concentration, on the pretext that the concentrated economy has greater power to multiply employment, even indirectly. This misconception stems from several reasons, among them - the fact that the exclusion indices of the concentrated economy are higher than the employment indices it creates, even indirectly; it also stems from the fact that the results of the concentrated economy tend to be reinvested in new initiatives to compete more, and therefore to concentrate more, making the circle of exclusion permanent. Only a revision of concepts, in the sense that it is not necessary to concentrate in order to grow, will be able to overcome this misconception.

The principle of deconcentration, therefore, is not aimed at centralized production or concentrated income and deconcentrated consumption - which has become a support and channel for further concentration. But it does aim to deconcentrate the production processes, where real income is created, so that, once income is broadened, consumption can increase as a consequence. This is true for people as well as for countries, both of which are often induced to consume, before the results of investment in production are promoted and reaped.

There is no universal recipe for policies to create and increase deconcentrated income. Such policies will have to be defined in each place, according to the characteristics of each moment, or each circumstance - the natural and human resources available, cultural realities and other factors.

However, and somewhat based on the Brazilian reality, the following are forms of job creation and increase of activities that allow the creation of more work places: the introduction of technologies at a rate that is not higher than the capacity to adapt, recycle and absorb labor; and the form of organization of companies, or production units that, instead of excluding, include, associate, humanize. This is possible.

It goes in this direction according to the book The Revolution of the Third Millennium (I):

- Support for the creation and development of small and micro-enterprises;
- The promotion of cooperative organisations of a solidarity, community, traditional or other associative nature;
- Continuous and parallel retraining in the innovation process to permanently prepare the workforce to absorb new technologies;
- The preparation of people in the education system and by other means, making them capable of managing work, a preparation that leads them to identify opportunities and to take advantage of them provides the conditions to transform these opportunities into work-creating enterprises;
- The adoption of effective government and social policies to give these parts of the population the conditions for access to the instruments required by these initiatives, changing a whole social structure and organization, which today favours concentrated activities and groups.

These changes call for a new culture and new norms, covering legal, financial management and other aspects, which make it possible to broaden access to ownership, credit, commercial channels, technology, modernization of management and, finally, which produce a real revolution in the norms, rules and behaviour that govern production companies and favour concentration. Legal norms and those that regulate the financial sector must therefore move in the direction of promoting participation instead of exclusion; multiplication of initiatives, pluralism and deconcentrated growth instead of concentration: broadening instead of excluding. In terms of government, it is along these lines that social policies are made possible and, in terms of business, this is how society becomes largely productive, markets expand and "we arrive at the society of the first world".

It is also important to pay attention to the fact that, in addition to new forms of organization that enable or promote inclusion, there are also sectors that are particularly suitable for increasing work opportunities and raising income in a decentralized way, among them:

- Rural development, whether sophisticated and entrepreneurial or family-type, which implies the development of a broad agrarian reform, i.e. it is not limited to access to land, but involves the provision of infrastructure for production, credit, training, extension services and the organization of distribution and marketing systems. In Brazil, an agrarian reform that also involves a policy of occupation of the sustainable land and organized and assisted migration, deconcentrating the country, further reduced to the occupation of one third of its territory - the country of the Treaty of Tordesillas 1942;

- To encourage handicraft activity which is not only considered as traditional and poorly paid work, but as an instrument of income generation, with a high human content, through art and cultural expression, and whose markets, in a world tired of anonymous and mass produced products, are in continuous expansion;

- The development of the service sector, mainly related to culture, leisure and improving the quality of life;

- In this line, tourism-related activities stand out, especially ecotourism, mystical and adventure tourism, which lead to the discovery of new dimensions of man, the world and nature, and allow employment opportunities to spread in a distributed way.

For this set of initiatives, and many other similar characteristics, the new social organization must promote an adequate legal and financial structure, especially focused on access to capital goods, forms of financing and technical assistance systems, human resource training and the development of other initiatives that allow the deconcentrated structure of the economy. According to this strategy, a choice of values, a vision of priorities and a new political consciousness are absolutely essential, because otherwise nothing happens, and things - profit, concentrated wealth that is useless - or useful to the interests of trade, war and domination, will continue to prevail over man, excluding and unbalancing the process.

It should also be considered that deconcentration should not be confused with simple decentralization or welfare. Decentralization means the diffusion or transfer of goods or power, created and owned in a concentrated manner, to lower levels or marginalized or excluded sectors of society, and therefore constitutes only one form of well-being. Deconcentration, therefore, does little to develop peripheral areas, or the bases of the social structure, contributes little to the effective strengthening of participation, pluralism of social organization and even less to the growth of empowerment or freedom. On the contrary. Sometimes decentralization, as a concession of concentrated nuclei, can contribute to the strengthening of concentration insofar as it legitimizes it as almsgiving and welfare, something that can be withdrawn in the same way as it has been conceded.

It is a mistake to imagine that concentrated growth - growth of the cake, as it has become commonplace to say - will return to the peripheries in a second phase.

This is only a half-truth, because the return, if it arrives, will be out of phase and proportional: it adds 10 to the concentrated system and 5 or 2 in the peripheral areas, thus increasing the imbalance, dysrhythmia and unsustainability of the process.

If the process were static and stratified, as assumed by the cake theory, there would, according to this conception, be progress. But since the process is dynamic, the concentration increases in geometric progression, and the return, or distribution in arithmetic progression, and that is the question.

Finally, it should be considered that economic deconcentration also covers aspects of the global economy, since the phenomenon of concentration in this era of globalization occurs at this level as much or more than at the internal levels of local societies or countries, as we have seen. Concentration is developing at an accelerated rate, and the numbers and the pace of this growth have already been analysed. Therefore, designing or introducing mechanisms for change at the internal or local level is not enough. Mechanisms to reverse the concentration-exclusion process - must also be adopted on a global scale.

An important role in this line must be played by international bodies, world conferences, summits, as the growth of the mass of consciousness, whose effectiveness, however, requires creating and proposing viable and effective models that must be developed and gain space in this world of interdependence, by all means offered by technology.

The **union of** emerging countries and their influence **on** excluded countries may prove to be a decisive factor in this change. Organizations such as the Group of 20, some agreements between emerging countries, already proposed or made effective, show that this is possible, although there is a lack of alternatives and operational proposals.

Signs that this is possible are also spread throughout society:

- The feelings of those who perceive the necessity and possibilities of the new era or the new post-technological society;
- In so many others who, even if in a romantic or emotional way, are looking for other ways to organize themselves, live and coexist;
- In cultures that traditionally adopt principles of participation and renunciation or limitation of ambition, cited as principles of wisdom inspired by the essential culture or ethic, or by ancestral tradition - principles that can be adopted and applied with necessary adaptations, if any, for the post-technological era. What is happening is that now, with the same principles, technology can be adopted and the new civilization - the synthetic civilization - can be organized, without the new society running the risk of falling victim to its own technology, or continuing under the threat of being out of step with the evolution of the process over time.

Demographic deconcentration and occupation of empty territories.

Following in the footsteps of the concentrated economy, the population also tends to focus on seeking the benefits that the concentrated economy offers, or appears to offer. Parallel to this call, there is a growing lack of conditions, or support, to set and promote the development or improvement of the economy. living conditions in the empty surfaces or territories on the planet and with a great capacity to administer wealth. These territories, if not occupied in favour of the inclusion process, will end up being occupied by the interests of concentrated systems, or even on the argument of the prevalence of global interests over local interests, or sovereignties and other arguments that will never fail the wolves.

The case of the Amazon and the Brazilian savannahs is a typical example of the planetary interests and dimension of this issue. These are 5 million km2 of territory, endowed with immense resources, which are not even measured or used rationally, and therefore threatened with disorderly and predatory exploitation for the benefit of the few, or those who control the systems - the new colonizers, who will thus continue to expand their domains and impose their criteria for ordering the world.

In addition, there are inadequate or insufficient policies capable of determining rationalized forms of urban growth, generating the swollen cities that are characteristic of underdeveloped countries in particular. Of the cities with more than one million inhabitants, the absolute majority are concentrated in poor, underdeveloped countries, without wealth, work opportunities or urban facilities capable of overcoming or preventing the swelling that necessarily produces this disorderly attraction.

The phenomenon of concentration of populations occurs, in fact, in two directions, according to the analysis made in "**The Third Millennium Revolution**":

One, by the demand for population flows from rural areas or small towns to urban areas, the largest cities, the origin of the megacities, which, for the most part, in emerging and underdeveloped countries, are nothing but immense illusions or lost dreams because they offer no human living conditions for these flows. These cities are swollen, formed by excluded peripheries and dehumanized life, where people lose their identity, their values, their landmarks; where misery spreads, and violence increases in volume - two types of violence: the struggle for survival and the conditioning of systems, which use the inhuman conditions in which people vegetate to exploit them in every way.

The other determining direction of these population flows, which urban imbalances produce, is mainly the result of the abandonment of vast regions, relegated to a minimum of physical, material and social infrastructure. Overcoming this abandonment would require broad policies aimed at attracting people to settle in these areas, or being able to retain those who reside there, making them productive, participatory and integrated into the processes of continuous improvement of the quality of life (human development).

The occupation of these territories would make it possible, on the one hand, to evacuate excessively concentrated areas, or to interrupt the continuation of this process of concentration, and on the other hand, to promote new opportunities for growth and to increase work, employment and income opportunities. Once this environment has been created and the deconcentration of the population allowed through these consciously adopted policies, people tend to be less excluded or marginalized, they will be better able to find themselves, maintain their cultural identity, integrate with nature or the environment and its values, and finally participate in the post-technological society or the new civilization.

Countries which, for historical and other reasons, have managed to occupy their territories in a balanced manner, have also achieved more harmonious forms of development and social organization internally. Poor countries find it more difficult to achieve this harmony, as a result of their own poverty, which denies them the resources to promote policies leading to balanced territorial and demographic occupation. Sometimes they also lack the perception, preparation or competence to perceive the importance of these policies. The consequence of this incapacity is the formation of another vicious circle of concentration and exclusion.

It should be considered, however, that the density of this occupation and its territorial distribution, demographic occupation, does not, in itself, produce an absolute index of well-being, participation or quality of life. The results of territorial occupation or territorial demography remain directly related to social, environmental, physical and social conditions, appropriate infrastructure to make it sustainable. If these conditions are met, deconcentration will tend to consolidate and produce results. If not, it will tend to intensify exclusion and flight to urban centers, swelling them and accentuating the imbalances in the process.

However, such policies are possible and have been successful where they have been applied. I cite as an example the process of developing a deconcentrated model of social organization - of the economy, of population distribution and of territorial occupation, a model that has been consciously improved, which has totally changed the conditions of backwardness of a Brazilian state in relation to other units of the Federation. This state, where the principle of orderly deconcentration is applied, has become, in a few decades, one of the states with the best quality of life, or human development, in the country.

In the 1960s, of the previous century, the state of Santa Catarina was a small (by Brazilian standards) state in the south of Brazil, which the indicators designated as the poorest in that region, compressed between the large states of Rio Grande do Sul, Paraná and São Paulo, with their capitals transformed into large poles of concentrated national or regional development - Porto Alegre, Curitiba and São Paulo.

Throughout this decade, a debate has taken place in the state to determine whether they should adopt a development model based on investments concentrated in the capital, Florianópolis, to compete with the rich neighbouring states and their capitals through a new pole, or whether they should opt for the promotion of deconcentrated investments, strengthening each of the state's regions and integrating them with each other, through an articulated system of transport and infrastructure.

This conception prevailed, which inspired the **Santa Catarina development project** in the early 1970s, proposed by the state government[23] and assumed by the Santa Catarina society -- entrepreneurs, intellectual elites (there are now 12 regional universities, absorbing about 170,000 young people and promoting regional knowledge and its global integration), the political-administrative organization, and finally, the clear awareness of the choice adopted as "Santa Catarina's development model".

Today - 40 years later, the state of Santa Catarina presents, among the Brazilian states, the best and greatest indices of balance, quality of life and human development, as demonstrated, beyond the statistics, by the increasing population flows from other parts of the country that come to the state, not only for tourism, but to settle there. In fact, the stage of development reached and its characteristics have been the result of a territorial policy of territorial, demographic, economic and social occupation, deconcentrated, based on infrastructures well distributed throughout the state territory and properly articulated.

The case of Santa Catarina contrasts with the situation in most Brazilian states, which concentrate or let concentrate and have swollen their capitals, creating shantytowns, damaging the environment and promoting exclusion. Moreover, this is also the case in Brazil, and the exclusion indices already analysed prove it. The process is repeated, especially in underdeveloped countries: the process of concentration and exclusion -- which deteriorates the quality of life, depersonalizes people, creates poverty and misery, in contrast to what happens in countries with a spatially and socially well-distributed population.

Devolved society indeed implies the development of immigration policies, a demographic and territorial organisation. However, local and regional migration

---

[23] Salles, Colombo Machado - Catarinense Development Project. S. c. State Official Press - 1971.

policies are not enough, since the same imbalance in demographic distribution and the causes behind it are global in nature. The same policies must therefore be the subject of supra-national strategies, aiming at a better correspondence between wealth and occupation of territories and so that migratory flows do not seek only concentrated and developed territories, increasing imbalances and repeating, in a global dimension, the same illusion of those who seek capitals or concentrated poles and who concentrate, internally. In these areas, migrants find themselves isolated and excluded from the developed societies where they have sought a place, creating new imbalances and new situations of exclusion, real economic and social ghettos, with new caste structures that are strengthened by sharing society into first and second category human beings.

The deconcentration of knowledge, technology and culture.

The post-technological age is essentially the age of knowledge -- the phrase that, expressing truth, without losing force and content, can become a commonplace. Anthropologically, this fact shows that the human species overcome, not only in the physical, or technological, but in the essential, or consciousness in its broadest sense, stage of raw matter, weight, form, or mass (in physics), as well as wealth, pre-potency, violence, conflict, and the hold of the strongest over the weakest (in the psychological, sociological, or ethical realm), for new, lighter -- more spiritualized forms of life: knowledge, the search for transcendence, mysticism or spirituality; access to cultural goods and leisure, which finds its counterpart in solidarity and cooperative forms of coexistence; peace, instead of war; participation rather than exclusion ; cooperation instead of competition; solidarity and love instead of selfishness and conflict; quality of life, or finally, humanization, well-being and happiness, or **being more, instead of** simply **having more**, accumulating more, and excluding.

In the context of the knowledge age, technology can -- and should -- be transformed, as a necessary corollary, into an instrument to enable these new values to organise post-technological society according to them, rather than being used as an instrument for consolidating society and traditional values, thereby exacerbating imbalances in the process.

Is the necessary choice, then, to maintain the concentration or monopoly of knowledge, technology and culture, which is contrary to the nature of the evolutionary process, or is it to respond to the essential vocation of this process, the path of deconcentration, which makes possible and produces pluralism and freedom? The monopoly of knowledge, in fact, in addition to being associated with other ethical factors, responsible for exclusion, becomes unsustainable because it contradicts the nature of the process, even if technology makes it possible to preserve it and prolong its survival.

This also leads us to reconsider the principle, already made explicit, that not everything that technology makes possible can be done; on the contrary, technology must be used to make possible what must be done.

Thus, it can be said that the technology allows for more sophisticated forms of killing than traditional forms -- lethal injection instead of hanging, or hunger and malnutrition, rather than the power of life and death over the slave. Or electronic warfare, which kills from a distance, anonymously, without eye to eye, as when sword, rifle or bayonet were used to kill.

This is not to say, however, that murder becomes ethical, or less illegal.

Similarly, it can be said that technology makes it possible to concentrate and, by concentrating, to exclude and, by excluding, to produce misery, hunger, malnutrition and death. But just because it allows concentration does not mean that we can use technology to concentrate and exclude, maintaining a model of systems which, by excluding, allows the death of millions of people, the destruction of the planet or the breakdown of the process, and this too we have already seen.

In fact, it is because we avoid establishing the strict and close relationship that exists between the system that excludes, and by excluding, produces misery and hunger -- that we condemn ourselves; and concentration, an ethically and legally acceptable form of organization, because it produces the profit and wealth of a few, at the price of the growth of the excluded. For these reasons, there is resistance to inserting the ethical question in the analysis of the current model and in the maintenance of the monopoly of knowledge, technology and culture, like the other factors of imbalance in the process.

In reality, while economic concentration excludes men from material goods, the concentration of knowledge, technology and culture denies them access to the goods of conscience, to spiritual goods, and therefore constitutes a matter as serious or more serious than economic concentration, even though, like Siamese sisters, all forms of concentration are inseparable, aligned with each other.

Finally, it must be considered that the deconcentration of technology must be used to disseminate knowledge and promote cultural diversity, to be recognized as belonging to a pluralist and free society. In this context, the new social institutions, based on ethics and law, must ensure access to knowledge and diversified cultural production; they must limit the monopoly of technology and the means that it makes viable, by giving precedence to the right to access and participation over the absolute right to property.

Just as the interests of society or the rights of individuals impose limits on the right of ownership of material goods -- which is already recognized, for example, when the principle of the prevalence of the social function of property is affirmed -- the same interests of society impose limits on the monopoly of knowledge and its use -- technology, or its product -- culture, according to the rights inherent in human nature.

In this context, it is adapted to the new civilization, although only small steps have been taken in line with this reasoning, for example, the right to infringe patents on essential medicines, which is beginning to be recognized in international forums. This example, however, needs to be amplified in scope and content, in order to transform technology into an instrument of human participation and inclusion in society caused by its own technology.

Making technology an instrument of concentration is a procedure that runs counter to the nature of the process of civilization, and thus to essential ethics. The same can be said of the use of technology to eliminate cultural identity and diversity, for it is this identity and plurality that underlie ordered complexity, that is, once again, freedom, dignity and human fulfilment.

Political deconcentration.

Politics in the context of this analysis is concerned with the organization of power in society and how that power is exercised.

Political deconcentration refers to the reduction of concentrated power, at the top of society, or, from another point of view, to the growth of power at the base of social organization, where people are and the groups that are most connected to it, sociologically called "face-to-face groups". Deconcentrated power thus reinforces people's autonomy, participation and ability to influence the exercise of power, i.e. the decisions and actions that affect them. It therefore limits the threat of state prepotency, which often materializes when power is exercised far from people. Here, power tends to be exercised on the basis of objectives unrelated to the well-being and promotion of people, which are themselves replaced by the state, the ruling group, or even by other myths, such as money, power per se, when it is not the nation, or race, as the Nazi and fascist states did.

The source of the power of the state must also be considered to be the persons, or the corporation, and that power is legitimate to the extent that the corporation has delegated it to the state. In other times, it was believed that power came from God.

In any case, only dictatorships believe that their own state is the source of power. The exercise of power, therefore, beyond the limits and delegation of society is ethically indefensible and should be legally indefensible. Depending on the delegation it assigns to the State, the corporation may keep parts of the power for itself, or it may delegate it to third parties other than the State. Therefore, it is also ethically and legally unacceptable for the state to assume or attribute to itself the status of sole representative of the corporation. The power of the State is only legitimate and ethical, and therefore constituted as a "State governed by the rule of law", by the free and sovereign delegation of society, within the limits of this delegation.

In this context, it is important to understand clearly that in democratic societies, individuals or societies can be represented and effectively represented by many social institutions, to which they transfer functions, parcels of power inherent in them. The legitimacy of this transfer results from the freedom that is inherent in the nature of the free and rational beings that make up society. The State, which grants itself the monopoly of social representation, usurps delegation and transforms itself into a totalitarian State, even when it calls itself a social State, a socialist State, or camouflages the usurpation committed with equivalent expressions. The error of socialisms stems from the idea of replacing society by the arbitrator of the State, transformed into its sole arbitrator representative, speaking on his or her behalf, defines rights, imposes obligations and duties, and even concedes power, in the measure of his or her own interests, reversing the equation.

Historically, the origin of this error or confusion between the social state and the socialist state can be attributed to the theory of the "dictatorship of the proletariat" that would assume power to impose society "collectivist", and would dispense with the existence of its own state. Collectivism - the actual socialist society, however, is still only a theory. In practice, exactly the opposite would happen.

The "dictatorship of the proletariat," like any other dictatorship, exercised in the name of any interest--any class, any ideology, even a utopia, has crystallized the state, transforming it into a totalitarian state. In its softened forms, socialism maintains the interventionist state, sometimes hidden as a social state. These errors explain the confusion that is made between socialism, which is really linked to society, and socialism, which is linked more to the state than to society, self-investing as the sole representative, even if it does not always represent society . And that, above all, it does not always respect society itself, or man, as the object and origin of all rights.

Political deconcentration of the power structure, therefore, has nothing to do with the socialist state. Political deconcentration means the distribution of power by the social body, not the strengthening of the power of the state. Political deconcentration claims that people can effectively participate in power, not only in its constitution, or origin, but in its exercise.

In short, political deconcentration does not mean any form of delegation of state -- or central power -- granted, as a privilege, to the social body, or to parts of society. The deconcentration of power, so conceived, often turns into an instrument to reinforce central power, now as a conceding power, or origin of social power, reversing the nature of the process.

Concretely, the deconcentration of power, if it is to be effective and consistent with a pluralist, free and effectively democratic society - the necessary counterpoint to the totalitarianism of the state, must take two directions:

- **Horizontally** - by reducing single-person power according to multiple forms of participation, or collegially - a more representative form of persons or society. This participation generally occurs through its segments (parties -- parties) organized. In this case, it can be said that parliamentary forms of government, considered theoretically, because they are more horizontally deconcentrated, are more legitimate as instruments for the exercise of power, than the unipersonal forms, which were expressed in other times by monarchies or absolute governments and today by presidentialism;

- **In the vertical direction** - by diminishing central power and the growth of power at the source, or on the basis of social organization, among its members and in social groups. Vertical deconcentration makes possible the effective participation of people, their presence and influence in decisions, their control over actions, and finally, the exercise of individuality, responsibility and freedom, sometimes summarized in the word citizenship, although citizenship represents much more.

According to this conception, it is from individuals and groups that power is transferred through various forms of delegation to intermediary organisations in general, constituting society, and to organisations, particularly political organisations, constituting the State. It also follows from this conception that the powers of the groups or intermediary organizations must prevail over the central power. One could say, as a principle of political organization, that the powers of the municipality -- closer to the people -- must be strengthened in relation to the powers of the states, or federal units, in Brazil, and these levels of power must be strengthened in relation to the central state.

In short, municipal and federative forms of political organization of the state are more compatible with the principle of deconcentration than unitary, imperial, or centralized forms of organization.

Just as the principle of deconcentration applies to the structure of the State, it also applies to other political entities, political parties, in the first place, because of their importance and role in political organization. However, they must cover all kinds of bodies and institutions that exercise parcels of power over society, or that serve instrument to these plots. Thus, the principle of political deconcentration applies not only to the executive, but to the legislature and the judiciary and to all those vested with parcels of power.

This is the direction in which the evolution, and therefore the reforms of political structures in the post-technological society are moving, making possible the participation of people so that the concentration of power, reinforced by technology, does not become one more system to oppress society, kill diversity and exclude people, creating another form of imbalance and the unsustainability of the process.

In conclusion, we should also reflect on the new forms of power over national States, which are exercised by international organizations and the formation of blocs, also through other associative forms of States and corporations in all fields. The importance of these new forms of power is becoming ever greater, constituting a new fact that goes far beyond traditional alliances. Traditional alliances have not had much to do with what is happening today with supranational powers or structures.

These new organizations are compatible with the era of globalization, but only when transforming domestic affairs, the global national interest in global issues, which emphasizes commitments to interdependence and mutuality and broadens relationships in the pursuit of cooperation, consensus and harmonious coexistence among nations.

This service and these new organizations are positive channels for cooperation, but they cannot go beyond consensus and are absolutely superimposed on the organizations that join together to form them. Otherwise they would turn into new forms of global totalitarianism. This balance is difficult to achieve, but it is in this way that supranational institutions gain in effectiveness and legitimacy.

Respect for sovereignties, cultural diversity, political regimes, ideologies and other forms that characterize pluralism and ensure the maintenance and exercise of freedom are therefore essential elements in legitimizing this new order in the making. This means that, in this new order, the principles of cooperation, participation and the coexistence of common interests, which lead to solidarity and participation -- such as the principle of pluralism, which guarantees the exercise of freedom -- must be considered as essential values to be constituted.

It is in this construction, more than in the control of the interests of competition and concentration, that this new level of human relations can contribute to the viability of the political structures of post-technological civilization.

The globally deconcentrated company.

From all of the above, one can get an idea of how deconcentration should cover the entire social organism and shape it in all its expressions, promoting the strengthening and multiplication of social organizations at the base of society and throughout its body.

The family group is the centre of this structure, forming the basic fabric of all this multiplicity of organizations and institutions that express the diversity of forms in which people organize themselves to play their multiple roles. Biologically, the development of techniques and new possibilities for the production or multiplication of living beings, including humans, can apparently diminish the role of the family. In sociological, psychological, cultural and spiritual aspects, however, which means in intrinsically human aspects, even if the possible repercussions of the biological aspects are not weighed, nothing has developed, and probably nothing will be developed to replace the family group with an advantage for individual development and for the evolution of the human species.

Notably because, when these levels are affected, we begin to move beyond the dimensions of technology to other human, ethical, or essential dimensions beyond biology and genetic engineering.

For these reasons, given the complexity of human nature and social processes, and the ethical compromise between being and the nature of things, a pluralistic and deconcentrated society presupposes, at least at this stage at least, and certainly on a permanent basis, the strengthening of the family group in order to play its multiple roles in the most diverse planes of life, providing support, reference and guidance to people from childhood to old age. Affectivity, the system of relationships, the maturing of love are not parts or products that can be mass-produced, as long as technology is developed.

In order for the multiple social roles of individuals to be more fully developed, however, their circumstances -- returning to the expression of Ortega y Gasset -- must be organized outside the family group.

According to the assumption that the evolutionary process materializes as a process of ordered complexification, it is deduced that the more society evolves, the more functions it requires, and therefore the more social institutions necessary for the full exercise of these functions increase.

Minimizing these functions, reducing their quality or quantity, and handing them over to the state, or to groups that concentrate and monopolize them, therefore goes against the nature of the process.

The weakening of social organizations, the monopoly of functions, going against the nature of the process, the move towards an increase in imbalances, the loss of pluralism and thus the conditions for the exercise of freedom, that is to say the construction of a truly human civilization.

In the conception of the complex, ordered and pluralist, and therefore structurally free and fully humane society, it is necessary to multiply the forms of social organization, and to recognize them in the legal structure, according to their nature. For this, legal recognition of state groups is not enough -- according to the presupposition that they represent society, and private groups representing individuals. It is important to increase efforts and initiatives aimed at giving a legal nature to social beings, parts of society that organise themselves as autonomous collective beings in relation to the state and individuals. This conception will diversify and strengthen social structures, widening the space for pluralism and freedom.

To this multiplicity of social bodies that are autonomous from the State and from individuals, some rightly call the third sector, as opposed to the first -- individuals and the insured -- the State. In practice, however, since it constitutes an innovation in the legal concepts of being, there is some difficulty in strengthening it, recognising it as truly autonomous, a key instrument of structurally deconcentrated society.

The evolution of the process, or human creativity, however, will eventually overcome the traditional dualism expressed in culture and as in legal norms, of recognizing only the existence of the individual or the State. The new civilization will open space for recognizing society, which is the expression, extension and essential circumstance of man and his system of relationships.

New social institutions

This set of institutions -- the third sector -- will shape the post-technological society, and will give greater expression to the aspirations of the mass of consciousness in all areas of the social structure, i.e. in the political, economic, legal, ethical, educational fields, wherever the aspirations of the emerging, pluralistic, participatory and supportive society, i.e. the fully humane society, may be found. Non-governmental organizations, created by society, the so-called Non-Governmental Organizations, among other forms of association, are multiplying in Brazil and in the world. Organizing and representing society and replacing the State in many of its functions, these institutions carry out the most varied activities, expanding social participation and empowering individuals and society to be present as active agents of the process. In this way, the space of society that the State has occupied is recreated.

Until there is, however, a clear affirmation of the proper identity of these institutions, however, as society organizes itself -- exercising the right to organize itself, the state bureaucracy -- which always judges itself to be the owner and lady of society, its institutions and often people, it will always tend to regard them as if they were government agencies. Or as if they were private organizations. It seeks to justify the continuation of this dualistic and reductive view as a precaution against the possible abuses that may occur on the part of these institutions.

But, by any chance, hasn't the state itself always been prodigal and its bureaucracy to commit abuses of all kinds? Could society not use its own mechanisms for these controls, with greater efficiency and legitimacy than the State itself does?

In any case, regardless of how these and similar institutions, which are truly representative of society, are organized, they will multiply in all its segments, throughout the world. In this way, they are beginning to constitute indispensable instruments for responding to the growing complexity and plurality of social structures and functions, helping to overcome the monopolistic tendencies inherent in concentrated systems, whether corporate or State, the instruments of monopolies and concentration.

But it is not only NGOs and other forms of association that are characterized as social institutions necessary for pluralist, free and fully humane social organization. There are tens or thousands of other deconcentrated institutions that strengthen the social structure and therefore need to be strengthened. These are educational institutions, devoted to the field of education; clubs of all kinds with the most diverse objectives in the fields of leisure and culture; the Churches, in their multiple manifestations, in the religious field; groups that develop, focused on reflection, philosophy, the development of science, or the search for mystical or spiritual experiences ; service clubs and welfare organizations; cooperative organizations, trade unions, small and micro-businesses -- as well as medium and large enterprises, as long as they are not monopolistic; and finally, a number of organizations which, the more diverse and numerous they are, the more they reflect a complex and evolved society where there is room for participation and solidarity. In contrast, closed and systemized societies become poorer as a society the more monolithic they are.

Finally, it should be noted that the multiplication of social groups, both primary and intermediate, does not remove the efficiency of society. This argument is still used in favour of monopolies and concentrated organizations. However, deconcentrated societies can become more productive overall, which does imply, it is true, that they must be adequately prepared to absorb, adapt and use technological advances. Its effectiveness lies in the fact that in this way, exclusion will be reduced and the whole social body will be integrated into the process, rather than reinforcing a centre or a single machine, which will have to drag an inanimate and shapeless body along.

Several examples have been analysed previously, that cooperative and deconcentrated society is possible. I will now cite one example, in the economic field, where, in general, there is greater resistance to deconcentration, under the erroneous argument that only concentration is competitive and effective.

Despite the enormity of some mega-enterprises based in the Veneto region of northern Italy, more than 60% of its gross domestic product is generated by almost 70,000 micro and small enterprises, if we also consider that some large corporations operate in a deconcentrated manner, producing in small family or community units, in an efficient work integrated with their headquarters, which perform, in particular, the functions of management, planning and research and quality control.

Other examples of the effectiveness of business organizations working in associated systems can also be cited. In Brazil the integrated production model is often used in rural areas, particularly in the dairy and cereal sector -- the most significant examples are in the enterprises of the State of Santa Catarina, already mentioned as an effective model of deconcentration. This model generates a strong agro-industrial chain, which can inspire the outlines of the viability of a new, more modern project for the country, because it is more deconcentrated or participatory, cooperative and supportive.

Finally, it is worth noting alternative experiences, perhaps seeds for the future, or valid expressions of the principles of cooperation, participation and solidarity, such as the community cities that exist in different parts of the world. These are seeds inspired by the aspirations, though diffuse, of the mass of consciousness in the formation of utopias perhaps pushed to the extreme, but which show the possible limits of human coexistence, which will give rise to a new era -- a civilization in which the human being evolves, and society with him, in the sense of participation and solidarity in human relations and its organizations, replacing the era of competition, conflict, concentration and exclusion -- by the era of harmony and peace, as the only way to avoid rupture, giving sustainability to the process.

Is it too much to expect that man, recognized as capable of making the technological revolution, should also be capable of making an equivalent revolution in himself and in the institutions that make up his milieu -- or his circumstances?

1.3 COOPERATION AND SOLIDARITY.

Time to choose.

The consequences of the concentration model, which insists on surviving and imposing itself, dangerously aggravating local and global imbalances, and considering that competitors one by one are gradually being eliminated, make it clear that we are witnessing the end of the era of competition, which would lead us to the end of pluralism and freedom. From this point of view, the question only comes down to waiting to see who will be the last of the competitors in this gladiatorial arena.

However, unlike what happened in the Roman circus, when at the end of the competition, the spectators raised or lowered their thumbs, defining the show, at the end of this process, there will be a world to be seen rebuild. The best would be to build it before the end of the show, in the context of technology, with the strength and dimension of technology.

In this moment of reconstruction, or in this construction, technology and all that it produces and that should serve man and not the whims of the emperor -- the systems and myths produced threaten to produce every day greater concentration and exclusion, resulting in global imbalance. In the reverse process, to eliminate the threat, technology must now produce deconcentration, no longer being the instrument of competition and exclusion, becoming the instrument for the production of diversity and pluralism and making possible a participatory, free and united world.

This is the choice facing humanity at this moment in history. This choice presents us with two alternatives: that of the global growth of the mass of consciousness which irreversibly points the way to deconcentration and cooperation, that is to say participation and solidarity, especially because society, with its instinct for history, evolution or survival, perceives this path; or the other path -- that of concentration, competition and exclusion -- towards the rupture of the process, given that the rupture, this time due to globalization, or the dimension of technology, could, if it occurs, be instantaneous and global, as has already been said.

In summary:

Just as deconcentration, in the post-technological era, opposes concentration and exclusion, and allows participation, in the same way, cooperation is based on solidarity, inserting it into the process and allowing a new balance in social organization. The new balance will ensure the continuation of the process itself, which has led history to this crucial and challenging moment, and will make it possible for the future.

Contents of cooperation and solidarity.

It is in this dimension that cooperation implies the growth of coexistence relations brought about by a broad process (not only financial) of globalisation and interdependence, aimed at building a world that is sustainable because it is balanced, which means shared in an appropriate way. This point of view stems from the perception that the resources of the planet, used sustainably by technology, are sufficient to build this shared world, overcoming the irrational phase of its appropriation by only a small part of local or global society. In reality, why produce imbalance, insecurity and rupture through concentration and exclusion, if much greater results in terms of meaning and quality of life or human fulfillment can be achieved through cooperation, promoting new forms of communication and solidarity? It is these new principles, inserted into the global mass of consciousness, that inspire more and more people and institutions throughout the world every day, and show that there are objective conditions for promoting the necessary changes.

This alternative cannot, in fact, be seen as just a dream, or simply as an ethical question, conceived as a virtue. This alternative must be understood above all as a condition for the viability or survival of society as a civilization, that is to say as a human society. For this and for it to be an effective alternative, it requires a joint effort -- of Nations and States, of people and institutions -- to develop concrete and operational models and mechanisms of cooperation, which will be in accordance with the conditions and the time, transformed into new institutions, adapted to the post-technological era.

It is thus a question of society assuming the "globalization of responsibility" or the "global responsibility for the survival or construction of civilization", transforming this awareness into operational structures and mechanisms capable of covering human organization and relations at all levels. Because of the inseparability of these two concepts, it cannot be forgotten that this effort implies, in addition to the operational dimension, an ethical dimension that refers to the relationship between the processes of cooperation. and the duty of solidarity. The ethical dimension is necessary because it is inherent in the nature of the process, and because of the inevitable consequences of rupture, if the process continues to move in the opposite direction to nature, that is, in the direction of conflict and exclusion.

The rupture, if it occurs, should fall all the more on those who have accumulated everything, because those who are excluded, those who have nothing, or who, in the process, have found themselves with nothing, have little to lose.

Assuming the inevitability of this transformation, penetrating into the essence of the process and transforming it in order to adapt it to human nature and the nature of society and its dynamics, this is the challenge facing this generation, which must, in its short space of time, make the transformation of today's civilization, considering that at other times, changes in this dimension have been consolidated over generations or centuries and millennia of history. Such is the scale of the challenge, now imposed by the dimension of technology.

Finally, it must be observed that to build the post-technological society, to overcome the imbalances, the dysrhythmia of the process and to build sustainability, is a much more complex proposal than policing or controlling the world, simply managing the economy, controlling the currency, speculating on the market, or even eliminating inflation -- at the price, or not, of growth, amplifying and intervening in the markets, or controlling them, exercising charity or promoting welfare, while maintaining the mechanisms of exploitation, concentration and exclusion. Building civilization requires more than maintaining global interests or aligning with them, submitting to the norms imposed by systems or maintaining systems. As long as the horizons of those who lead processes are these, as long as balance sheets are balanced, as long as the poorest economies are squeezed, as long as unpayable debts are produced, as long as national identities are sacrificed and global systems are imposed, plurality, freedom and the process of civilization, or its viability, will run serious risks. Those who reduce crises to such a superficial view do not realize that the nature of crises goes far beyond these reductionist policies and postures.

In reality, crises are consequences and not causes of imbalances in the process. Acting on consequences -- control of the world, hunger and exclusion, without changing the structures or the nature of the process, it may even be a way of putting consciences to sleep, while maintaining this model, which manages unsustainable imbalances and which will neither overcome the crises nor make the necessary transformations in the context of the change of civilization.

Models of cooperation and solidarity.

The construction of a society based on cooperation and inspired by the ethics of solidarity, or the need for survival, is possible and gives highly effective results. Important steps in this direction are being taken by many people and institutions, but not always with a clear awareness of its meaning and the dimension that must be assumed, and therefore without a clear awareness that this is just one step on the long road of necessary transformations. Similar steps are given in the political framework, reaching supra-national spheres. As far as these levels are concerned, it must be stressed that these steps are not the point of arrival, but only the beginning of the same process of change in search of new systems based on cooperation and solidarity. But for this to happen, it is necessary that these measures replace the reductive vision of competitiveness and its consequences with new strategies of cooperation which they seek, in this way, to make possible the construction of the new society, in solidarity.

In the supra-national sphere, of relations between nations, we can cite as an example of the effectiveness of cooperation, the process of building the European Union. In this process, the richest countries have invested billions of dollars -- and continue to invest -- in order to achieve a minimum homogenization of the economies and life models of the bloc's components, thus ensuring the necessary balance of the system. This strategy of cooperation has produced results, but it is not easy to know whether these mechanisms are aimed at building solidarity, as the foundation of cooperation, or whether what inspires them is only the strengthening of competition.

It is necessary, for example, to draw attention to this important issue. If the goal is simply competition, instead of a step forward, it will only reinforce the vicious circle.
In any case, the steps taken and the results obtained show that cooperation is a possible and effective way to achieve concrete results.

Within the framework of people of solidarity and cooperatives, in which the ethical dimension predominates, we can highlight as an example the statistical data published by the Brazilian Institute of Geography and Statistics -- IBGE. According to these data, in Brazil, approximately 40 million people participate in one way or another in cooperative and voluntary activities, either individually or through solidarity organizations. This means that out of four people, or out of three adults, one transforms his or her awareness of solidarity into actions of solidarity and cooperation. If this number is extrapolated, it can be said that more than one billion people in the world have this same consciousness and are, or could be effectively guided by it. Perhaps there are many more.
It must be considered that this mass of consciousness, which is being transformed into cooperative and solidary action in the world, exists and develops alongside those who seek only results, profit, concentration and the accumulation of results, be they individuals or institutions.

There are tens, thousands of forms and programs through which society or individuals, individually or institutionally, commit themselves to this new vision of responsibility in the construction of a different society based on new values. These people and institutions are certainly the largest part of the people and institutions that go out into the streets in every corner of the planet to fight for peace, against exclusion and global imbalances, demanding transparency, justice and equity, that is to say, a new dimension, a human dimension for structures, procedures and social organization. It is a mistake to ignore or deny them.

Why the slowness to transform this consciousness and action into a new theory of social organization, appropriate to this consciousness, to the post-technological era, to human aspirations and to one's own survival of the process? **Why are churches, universities, communicators and the media at their disposal not sufficiently engaged in the formulation of this new theory and practice**, those who have the power to make laws or to judge procedures, those who govern, finally, all those who are accountable and take their share in the overall responsibility?

This is not a dream. This is not a utopia. It is the condition for the continuity of the civilizational process, so that the story of the dinosaurs, who one day also dominated the world, is not repeated. But we are not dinosaurs. Or are we?

These are also questions that cannot be killed.

1.4 - THE MASS OF AWARENESS AND THE MULTIPLICATION OF SOCIAL INITIATIVES.

All these processes, the cooperative organization of Nations, the social responsibility of people and institutions, forums and demonstrations for peace and the rejection of war, prepotency and exclusion, the growth of the feeling and actions of solidarity are manifestations and indicators that the mass of consciousness is developing in favor of the new society, the humanized society, or the civilization of the post-technological era.

Socially responsible companies.

In the same context, showing how the mass of consciousness is developing and being transformed into concrete facts, I now bring you the testimony of the press on a new ongoing process, which is gaining new dimensions every day: the growth of social responsibility of social enterprises and other organizations in Brazil and elsewhere in the world.

The report presented by the magazine Carta Capital -- Special Edition No. 270 of December 2003, informs that "of the 782,000 companies in Brazil, 462.00 declare that they are active in the field of social promotion. Contributions range from donations to the implementation of structured projects. (Remember, in particular, the 40 million Brazilians -- individuals who dedicate themselves, in solidarity, to volunteer work). The magazine develops the theme under the title **The Wave of Social Responsibility** and brings in concepts of this kind in its editorial signed by the renowned journalist Mino Carta, the magazine's chief director. The editorial aims to identify and reflect the feeling that is spreading in the business environment.

The capitalist world shows its social face, says the editorial of the Review

Much of the business community is beginning to understand that companies must go beyond the goal of generating profits and distributing them to their shareholders.
Society expects companies to treat the parties with whom they deal ethically as well. And that they account for the positive and negative effects generated in society from their production processes.
Pressures are increasing for appropriate management of natural resources -- in effect appropriate public goods in the production process -- and for reducing environmental impacts. This is a great opportunity for companies to get involved, alongside civil society, in the search for solutions to the country's deep social drama.[24]

This is a valuable testimony and these are concepts that deserve consideration, especially since they come from a magazine specialising in Capital or in Capitals, as its own title expresses it.

Then the magazine develops a comprehensive analysis of this exercise in corporate social responsibility and describes in a special framework various representative moments in the evolution of social responsibility in the corporate world, from the Second World War to the year 2003. On the other hand, the analysis of this evolution also shows the origin and growth of the mass of consciousness in the institutions, which runs through the whole process, sending us back to the pre-

---

[24]Carta, Mino Mario - Revista Carta Capital nº 270 - December 2003.

technological era of absolute profit, extreme socialism or liberal capitalism without limits and without social responsibility, until we arrive at today's consciousness.

Some of the latest facts quoted by the magazine:

*1960s - Anti-Vietnam War protests in the United States lead to civil boycotts in supermarkets of food products **whose manufacturers had a stake in the fighting**. The movement was the embryo of the boycott of stock exchange shares. American companies had to explain to society whether they were sponsoring the war with money or selling products to soldiers.*

***The** 1970s - the first social balance sheet. In France, as in Brazil, entrepreneurs are pressured to prove, **through "social balance sheets"**, that they respect human working conditions.*

***The 1980s** - the state, which sponsors all **the profits, goes bankrupt in** France and England. In Brazil, the military regime begins to be dismantled.*

***1983** - Portugal promulgates its social balance sheet law and obtains (company) denial reports, and the American Chamber of Commerce launches the **Eco** prize for social projects of companies.*

***1986** - Birth of the Foundation Instituto de Desenvolvimento Empresarial e Social (Institute for Entrepreneurial and Social Development) - now the Ethos Institute.*
- The Capital Market Disclosure Committee guides the publication of the social balance sheet, which shows data on companies' personnel management.

***The 90's** - Financial balance sheet with social balance sheet, begins to be disclosed.*

***1992** - Paradigm in the publication of balance sheets, Banespa - Bank of the State of São Paulo, publishes the social report as well as the financial demonstrations. The document talks about the company's activities in the society and provides data on the working atmosphere. In addition, the balance sheet presents information on the value added (production index and wealth distribution).*

***The Securities Commission** (CVM) guides the disclosure of value added.*

***The Brazilian Association of Capital Market Analysts** (Abamec) - now Apimec - becomes the first financial market entity to discuss the social balance sheet.*

***1995** - Adoption of **Belgian legislation -** Civil society committees create a law on social auditing and submit the text to Parliament, ensuring more legitimacy to the process.*

***1997 - Sociologist Herbert de Souza,** Betinho**, realizes** that economic power must be combined to solve the problem of hunger in Brazil. The sociologist meets with the CVM to draw up the first social balance sheet. The trade unions and the Ibase participate in discussions and public hearings and the balance sheet model is approved. Betinho wants companies to be obliged to publish the social balance sheet, a discussion, however, that continues to this day.*

***1998** - Social certification labels come into force.*

***The city of João Pessoa** (Paraíba) issues the Herbert de Souza label.*

***1999 - Abamec** establishes rules: only companies that publish a social balance sheet will be able to take part in its competitions.*

***1999** - An index of 16 socially responsible companies is published by the accounting firm Access Consulting. Social criteria weigh as much as financial criteria.*

***Candidates** who have more than 10% of their investments applied to tobacco, arms trade and alcoholic beverages are excluded.*

***From 2000 to 2003**: The ethical, anti-smoking, anti-gun and anti-alcohol background emerges.*

***2000**: **Rio Grande do Sul begins to** certify companies that publish their social balance sheets.*

__2001__: __The Ethical Fund - ABN__ begins the process of excluding companies that deal with tobacco, arms and alcohol. The fund's investments include only companies with a declared social balance sheet.

__2002__: Consideration is being given to the requirement to include social value in the balance sheet.

__2003__: __The São Paulo Stock Exchange__ launches the Social Investment Portfolio, covering entities in the third sector. The Social Bovespa allows the client to monitor the investment on the Internet. The site offers more than thirty projects selected for fundraising.

So far, the Carta Capital magazine executive...

That same year, in a pioneering way, some Brazilian universities - among them the Universidad del Sur de Santa Catarina - **Unisul** presented their Social Balance Sheet, reporting on the actions and resources that invest in the human development of its students and the regional community in which they operate.

A process deviation alert.

It is also this year that the President of Brazil, Luiz Inácio Lula da Silva, is invested with his powers, a metal worker who has reached the post of President of the Republic led to the presidency by a posture and preaching inserted in the context of this "mass of consciousness," the worker president launches a series of social programs, among them "Zero Hunger," which has had some international repercussion, as well as other proposals, such as the creation of an international fund to fight hunger and poverty.

However, the President's social proposal continues to be hampered by the maintenance of economic policy linked to global systems of speculation, which concentrate and exclude, as well as by the inability to produce a coherent proposal, in terms of a national project, arising from the social aspirations and the mass of consciousness that brought him to power. In any case, and in spite of the limitations or contradictions of the government, the fact reveals the strength of the mass of consciousness, always in search of a new social theory, which in the Brazilian case affects the government, making it conflictual and aimless, a new social theory that would be able to make the transformation, not only of welfare. Financial assistance, the lack of a consistent social theory or synthesis, adding to the conflicts or contradictions that arise from it, can lead to an extremely frustrating result, because it has killed hunger or even disease, but has not transformed the social order that concentrates and excludes. Perhaps it has even put consciences to sleep, which is exactly what global systems want, contrary to the imperatives of necessary change.

Finally, in 2003, the World Social Forum, an initiative born in Brazil as a counterpoint to the World Economic Forum -- of the rich countries -- went to India to show its globality. In this Asian country, as in Porto Alegre, about 100 thousand people from all parts of the world came together to call for the construction of a different world, an alternative to the monopoly of globalization, of speculative economy or finance and the systems they support, and for peace, participation and world solidarity. In spite of its lack of objectivity - the Lacking a new theory of change, or a new social synthesis with clear objectives and effective strategies, the World Social Forum also reveals the globality of non-conformism with regard to the permanence of the current model, concentration and exclusion, and the need to build the new civilization on the basis of new values.

This set of actions in the business world, in the political field and in the global society, demonstrate that the mass of consciousness is developing, going beyond the state of immobility that one wants to impose on history, based on the principles of competition and concentration, as if they could still prevail and be sustainable in the post-technological world; as if they could still organize the society or civilization of this new era.

The immediate results of these actions, however, are only relative, because there is a lack of a coherent theory and appropriate instruments to ensure their operation and because they focus on the effects, or consequences of the existing order and on combating its distortions, rather than on changing the concepts, foundations and structures that cause, produce and maintain these distortions.

It is necessary to overcome these concepts and go beyond assistance, just as it is necessary for the conscience of society to go beyond the stage of simply expressing its revolts and aspirations. Such attitudes, if they are not able to change concepts and order changes, can contribute to the strengthening of its gaps, produce the industry of poverty, the marketing of charity, or even the virtue of charity, showing the success of the concept of the economist Marcio Pochman, who speaks of the **fight against poverty within the system** as the "**strategy of domination of**

the bourgeois world of the end of the twentieth century, which already included the concept of social responsibility" -- a fear, moreover, previously expressed in the analysis of this trend. The economist then draws a parallel between this liberal attitude and current attitudes, which act on the effects and not the causes of poverty (exclusion) and, "**whose aim is to dominate the clientele politically, through the distribution of quotas**". **Churches, NGOs and companies** (in the case of Brazil, one cannot but add governments, political parties ...), **all politically reproduce the perpetuation of poverty, over time -- the** economist states again.

This can really happen if the denunciations, the aspirations and actions remain on the surface without penetrating deep into the causes that generate poverty -- or exclusion if we are unable to devise the theory, the alternative strategy and the instruments capable of producing and sustaining the new form of human, participatory and solidarity-based development.

A joint effort is therefore needed to bring radicality to the change, to eliminate once and for all the foundations that ordered the pre-technological era and to make operational the foundations that will build the new order of participation and solidarity. Only deconcentration and cooperation as operational instruments of organization and of society's way of relating make this aspiration possible.

The survival of systems (or mega-organizations).

In the context of the march of the world for the new civilization, deconcentrated and cooperative, or, ethically, participative and supportive, what place is left to the global systems, or mega-organizations, which today control the world and command the process?

Some considerations around the issue must be made, since in the civilizational changes that have taken place in the past, representative institutions, overwhelmed by change, have always been eliminated and, in general, with violence.

This break should not take place immediately, in the context of the new civilization and in the era of global power. In order to prevent this from happening, however, a strategy of occupation of space by new organizations, both deconcentrated and cooperative, capable of defining the essential structure or overall functioning of the new social organization becomes necessary.

The occupation of space by new organizations presupposes changes, or the adoption of certain basic concepts that stem from the reality generated by technology.

Thus some sectors of the economy -- among them the most important in the current order of concentration and concepts in force -- will tend to lose their economic value, to the extent that they will have to be transformed into social goods, on the same level as other social goods such as air, water and the environment, to which all human beings have the right of access. Products that correspond to this category are infrastructure goods, complementary to the environment: energy, transport, communications, information, among others. Some high-tech products, such as software, are beginning to be offered to society free of charge. Tomorrow, sustainable forms will be perceived and created to adopt the same concepts and procedures with regard to certain infrastructure goods, or essential to survival and the guarantee of human dignity.

In order for this transformation to be possible and to occur in accordance with the nature of the process, the concepts and methods of production of these goods need to be transformed and made available to society, and this is possible.

The socialist perspective, this objective was imposed by the intervention of the state, in whose hands the goods were placed.

In capitalist regimes, this has been sought through market saturation.

Neither of these alternatives achieved the result in the expected dimension. It is natural that they did not obtain it because more than distribution or participation, these initiatives were based one on the profit of those who own and manipulate, the other on the strengthening of the own state, the socialist profit that engendered "the dictatorship of the proletariat", that gave birth to the dictatorship of the party, or of techno-bureaucracy or simply dictatorship.

How, indeed, or what strategy should be adopted to reach the post-technological society with broad participation, at least in essential goods, cooperation and solidarity?

Initially, for this to happen, it must be accepted that the post-technological civilization of deconcentration (or participation) and cooperation (or solidarity) does indeed constitute a radical change or a revolution of a civilizing nature. The expressions radical change or revolution -- I repeat, are not to be understood in their traditional sense of confrontation or violence, but in their sociological sense, just as we understand the technological revolution, thus simply meaning a profound change.

It must then be considered that socialization -- providing society, not the State, with essential goods -- would derive from the need for survival of the process, which must be ensured by the reintroduction of the necessary balance, and by the growth of other demands, the satisfaction of which requires that the systems be addressed. But they, the systems, or the mega-organizations, will not have monopolies of essential goods in the post-technological society, as they do in the present order, generating concentration and exclusion, or imbalances in the direction of rupture.

In reality, even in the present conditions, it is a mistake to imagine that systems or mega-organizations are the masters of the world, especially if we perceive that there are alternatives to concentration and competition that exclude. The technology itself allows these alternatives insofar as it makes complexity, multiplicity, deconcentration and cooperation possible and their management if it is competent. The question is therefore not one of technology, but of perception, or of formulation and political will. It is also a question of the overall strategies of countries and segments excluded from the process, those who do not benefit from the order of concentration. Irreversibly, these strategies will continue to gain space and, by manifesting themselves in supranational bodies such as UNCTAD, the Group of 20, bilateral and multilateral agreements, to which must be added the support of bodies of high moral credibility, such as UNESCO, ILO and the United Nations itself, despite the manoeuvres of all the possible masters of global power, which go against history.

Finally, it must be considered that the excluded countries, some of which are so-called emerging countries and others that have not even reached this stage, are the lords of their immense potential, particularly in natural reserves of renewable and non-renewable resources, without which the world cannot survive, and the world that controls the systems cannot survive either, and therefore their concern to police the rest of the world -- those who own the resources.

Biological reserves are part of these natural resources -- biodiversity, environmental reserves -- fauna, flora, water resources, in addition to the traditional resources represented, for example, by territorial reserves, by oil or by minerals of all kinds, especially those of a strategic nature.

The world cannot survive without these resources, and they will be increasingly accounted for in global balance sheets, in the global economy, as the countries that possess them have become aware of themselves and the value they possess and are organizing themselves to promote the new global social order.

They are deluding themselves, those who control the fragile and volatile financial resources, if they imagine that they can, with them, buy or subdue the real wealth of the world. They are also deluding themselves of those who think they can control the world with their nuclear warheads or their threats against the institutionalized world order, the concept of Nations and their civilized ways of being, serving as an example to the United Nations. What has taken place or continues to take place in Vietnam, Afghanistan, the Balkans, Chechnya, Iran and Iraq shows that the equation is much more complex than policing, imposing and invading, as was the case in the past, from primitive times to pre-technological times.

The union of this potential or alternative power, or of the countries that hold it, even for reasons of trade or survival, can and will occur as the mass of world consciousness continues to grow, demanding an alternative.

To paraphrase Bill Clinton, don't let the rich fool themselves...

1.5 THE VIABLE STRATEGY.

Presuppositions of strategy.

It is certain that the profound change, the transition of civilization, will not come from the rich. Nor will it come from those who, benefiting from the current system, refuse to see its imbalances and even more so to investigate its causes and therefore the reasons for its unsustainability. This is nothing new in history on the part of the beneficiaries of the current systems, and there is no point in going back over this fact.

Neither will it come, simply, from the growth of the mass of consciousness, even if it is a major factor in bringing about change.

It will not come, finally, only from theories and proposals, as long as they are logical, rational and appropriate to the reality of the post-technological world, to the evolutionary process, or to the aspirations of the growing mass of consciousness.

It is necessary that the different factors of change, conscious of the alternatives and of their own potentialities, allow a common strategy, capable of promoting the new process, while those who have seen history happen, will move away... will move away, straight to the past.

Capitalism, in its double face -- the state of socialist regimes and the private of liberal regimes, produced the first world -- in fact the world that came first -- leading through all forms of colonialism, to extreme consequences, competition and concentration -- and exclusion as a corollary.

In isolation, or for many countries, there is nothing to deal with concentrated power.

However, because of its characteristics and potential, some countries are in a position to establish an alternative strategy, which could be based on other foundations -- those of deconcentration and cooperation (of participation and solidarity, according to the mass of global consciousness), rationalizing and sustaining diffuse aspirations, instead of repeating the foundations that have led the process to its current imbalances and the threat of global breakdown. These so-called emerging countries, leading the Third World, could be the inducers of the new civilization.

This would be possible and the only threat to this alternative process would be for these countries to insist on, or repeat the mistakes of the past, brought into the present, going against the path of history, instead of building history.

Dimensions and potentialities of the emerging world.

Among these countries, due to its characteristics and dimensions -- for this and other cultural and historical reasons -- Brazil could articulate other emerging countries in deepening their influence on this process.

These are 8.5 million square kilometres, two-thirds of which are to be occupied -- the Amazon and the central-western part of the country, where there are natural resources to be exploited -- to be exploited in a sustainable manner. These are resources of planetary dimension and interest.

If only 20% of this vast territory were occupied, there would be 180 million productive hectares available, provided that they were occupied in the right place and in the right way. This vast area could produce not only food for a hungry world -- and, above all, hungry for natural food -- but also green food. Studies and assessments on the use of the Amazon have shown that if this 20% of the land were used to produce bioenergy -- clean, renewable energy -- it could replace the world's oil -- non-renewable and polluting to excess.

It is also estimated that 30 to 40% of the planet's biodiversity, the raw material of the third millennium, can be found in this vast area to meet the demand for all kinds of products. It is also home to nearly 15% of the world's water resources, in a world where water is becoming scarce, in inverse proportion to the growth in its demand in the region, in the country and in other regions of the world.

And there is also the largest environmental reserve and the largest rainforest, whose destruction could have unimaginable consequences for the global ecological balance.

It is, finally, a reserve of raw materials of all kinds, including strategic ones, a reserve which is largely unknown, made up of raw materials which are scarce in the world and which, used for centuries mainly by the first world, are almost exhausted.

With regard to Brazil's contribution, particular consideration must be given to the size of its resources, which, as can be deduced, are truly global. But it must also be seen as a reasonable market of nearly 200 million people, whose culture is based on peace, solidarity and cooperation, the result of a tradition of harmony and humanitarian feelings, not always expressed in institutions, but essential to the way Brazilian society is organized -- tradition and feelings, therefore in perfect harmony with the global mass of consciousness and adapted to the new organization of the post-technological era.

However, even Brazil, which, for these and other reasons, can move political wills, represents little on its own. Nevertheless, it is growing in size, inasmuch as it can be added to other countries with the same or complementary potential.

In Asia, for example, China and India, in particular, with their huge market of nearly 3 billion people -- almost half of the world's inhabitants -- their age-old culture, their alternative values, their needs to be satisfied and their potentialities offered to the world. In Asia, too, the Arab world, with its cultures, beliefs and traditions, complemented by oil, which is an absolutely important element in the transition.

Finally, Australia, South Africa, Nigeria and the emerging countries of the Americas, such as Mexico and Argentina, among others, should be considered. This group of countries, between which some steps towards political and commercial rapprochement have already been taken, can develop strategies of mutual cooperation and mutual support, addressing complementary needs, and strengthening partnerships on an alternative path to the dollar, speculation and exclusion that oppresses them. A new European Union, emerging countries? That is not quite what is proposed, because it is not a new bloc to compete, but a strategy of cooperation for a new civilisation. Nor is it a new FTAA to consolidate the support of the oppressed for those who exploit them. These countries account for two thirds of the world's population. It is the world's largest market, irrespective of its income conditions. It has the largest reserve of productive areas; it is home to the largest reserve of biodiversity, representing fauna and flora resources that do not exist in the first world. The same considerations apply with regard to water, productive territories, minerals, whether strategic or not, and the environment.

Finally, it is this emerging world that can strategically ensure the transition to the new civilization of the post-technological era.

We must consider that this is not a poor world, but a world reduced to poverty by the colonialisms of the past and by the continuity of a world order incompatible with technological advances and with the stage of the evolutionary process reached by the human species.

On the road to this agreement, there are difficulties of all kinds: interests, which will continue to be present; history, culture or ideology; traditions, customs and traditions that are different and sometimes contradictory. But if we look at the case of the European Union, whose countries, until the last century, fought in two world wars and today have managed to unite economically and politically, respecting individuality, cultural diversity and other characteristics of a plural, cooperative and supportive society.

Moreover, we cannot ignore the fact that this change will not happen today, in one day. But we must urgently start thinking about the future and start moving effectively in that direction. As the Chinese proverb says -- a march of a thousand steps begins with the first step. It can be said that some steps have been taken, others are still given, but there are many steps to give until the post-technological civilization is built, in which primacy:

- participation, the result of the devolution of goods of all kinds, which promotes inclusion and access, rather than exclusion ;

- solidarity, which is the fruit of cooperation, and which is produced by harmony, balance and security;

- peace, the fruit of participation and solidarity, the path or step that precedes love -- the love that moves the sun and all the stars in the vision of Dante Alighieri, amortizing the world, in the anthropological vision of Teilhard de Chardin, the love that sums up everything, the law and the prophets according to the ethics of Jesus Christ.

I know that these are not econometric expressions, nor are they significant perspectives on the so-called reductionist science, which translates complex realities into simple, or simplistic equations, and full or absolute realities into partial and small visions of reality.

But the reality is much greater, in spite of those who do not know where they come from and where they are going, entangled in their own -- and dangerous, "nonsense". Dangerous for themselves, for society, for humanity and for the planet, the home and dwelling of men.

Mechanisms for cooperation and inclusion.

Partnerships between emerging countries, which could be extended to other countries and which are seen as political and strategic reasons, could encourage the creation of common solidarity and cooperation funds, with a view to promoting development projects and processes with greater autonomy, greater use of local potential and values, transfer and dissemination of technologies and other inputs, making solidarity and cooperative instruments work effectively, rather than being dependent on mechanisms that impose recessive policies on them and pressurize fragile economies through exorbitant and unbearable burdens.

Examples of some of these mechanisms include the following. Moreover, some of them have already been proposed, and others exist, but without the dimension, objectives, or conceptual presuppositions that can give them the necessary effectiveness, as instruments of transition for the new society, the post-technological civilization.

A global food fund, for food production and distribution financed, or through exchange, or other mechanisms, including a sunset fund for the hungry world. The world, in this perspective, could produce more food instead of producing more weapons, for example.

A World Water Fund, aimed at the preservation and sustainable use of the planet's water resources, including for sanitation and supply programmes, especially in the poorest countries, eliminating one of the causes of the disease and misery that affects them.

A global environment fund, unifying several existing initiatives and proposals, among them the oxygen trade, and or the payment of royalties or taxes for the preservation of environmental reserves.

A global fund for literacy, dissemination of knowledge and forms of communication, development and access to appropriate technologies.

Finally, **a global emergency fund,** designed to assist and promote groups or nations in particular situations, that of extreme scarcity, which ensure for all, whatever the motive or argument, the minimum necessary for survival and the promotion of minimum humane living conditions.

One could still consider a cooperative and cooperative World Bank and investment or development bank for poor countries -- an alternative to the IMF -- which, rather than imposing generally spoliative and The Commission would support policies aimed at the use of resources and the development of local potentialities.

These funds would be made possible by the initiative of the poor or emerging, even if the rich and the masters of power resisted them, because the question is partly about resources, but it is mainly about awareness and choosing cooperation and solidarity.

1.6 - ETHICO-LEGAL CONCEPTION OF THE POST-TECHNOLOGICAL ORDER.

Ethics, practice and law.

Finally, it is important to consider that in this transition there must be an inseparable link between ethics, practice and law.

At this point, it is useful to recall the initial analysis that we are living in the moment of a passage of civilization and that we therefore have, in this generation, the opportunity to build a new social order, a new society or the civilization of the post-technological era, which has brought, among other new realities, globalization. In this new globalized world, the local dimensions are changing, or can rapidly take on absolute dimensions. It no longer makes much sense to think in a local or national order without its insertion in the globalized reality.

The foundations proposed for this new order, from an ethical point of view, can be summed up, as we have seen, in the concepts of participation and solidarity. These concepts summarize the essential aspirations, latent or explicit, in the mass of consciousness, which is constantly growing in the world. The essential content of the mass of consciousness is highlighted by the growing demonstrations in favour of peace, solidarity, participation, inclusion, pluralism and freedom, in opposition to war, conflict, competition, concentration, exclusion and totalitarian monopolies.

These dimensions, however, as long as they continue only in their ethical dimension, will not bring about the change of civilization. As we have seen, they find their practical content, their way of achieving it in practice, in the operational instruments of **deconcentration** and **cooperation**.

For this to happen, however, it is necessary to have a good understanding of the concept of ethics. It is also necessary, therefore, to design a new law -- the expression of the essential ethical concept, capable of regulating, in addition to the new issues raised by this transformed world, the foundations of participation and solidarity -- or of deconcentration and cooperation, giving them legal content and form, since it is the legal institutions that organize and express the structure and relations of organized society.

Essential ethics content.

I return to the Third Millennium Revolution. The book first defines ethics as the expression of conformity between reality and the nature of being and its relationships. It then defines **law as the** expression, or legal explanation of this conformity. According to this point of view, the question of the delimitation of the legal order -- thus of the expression of the ethical or participatory and supportive society -- is elaborated in the book as transcribed below, with some minor changes or additions that do not change, but only complete the contents already proposed.

The ethical foundations of participation and solidarity, made operational in practice through the instruments and mechanisms of deconcentration and cooperation, must inspire instruments capable of transforming and leading society in accordance with its nature, that is to say, as an organization that expresses the human condition, because we are talking about a society of men, human societies, and not about accounting, profit, money or the market. It is in this sense that operational instruments cannot oppose or ignore the ethical dimensions, i.e. their conformity with the nature of man and his organization in society. To do otherwise would be to fall into the same error of the current model of concentration and exclusion, which goes against the nature of man living and evolving in society. It would be essentially unethical.

For this reason, the proposed operational instruments are coherent, as long as they comply with the ethical content of the human process:

- Deconcentration expresses the ethical content of participation, an essential right that comes from human nature;

- Cooperation expresses the ethical content of solidarity, which stems from the bonds of union, complementarity and attraction that lead to love;

- The humanized society or the human process, finally in accordance with these essential contents, produces social balance or harmony and structural security, which generate or produce peace.

It is impossible not to mention this essential, or ethical, vision, according to the anthropological perspective proposed by Teilhard de Chardin, to say that all these elements have in amortisation of the world, the essence of its content, the love that allows the overcoming of all that separates greed, competition, concentration, exclusion, conflicts, hatred, war, and the parade of the beasts of the apocalypse that threaten the world, on the basis of the absolute, or global, dimension of the power of technology .

All reductionism will consider it unscientific to insert love as an instrument and element of social organization. Reductionism, which reduces man to a piece of the machine, does not realize how anti-scientific it is to analyze the body without the presence of the blood that vivifies it, or nature without the sap that nourishes it. Or not to see, even a little, beyond appearances.

We therefore conclude that the humanization of the world is only possible as they overcome primary instincts, replacing them with a new vision of values that represent the aspirations or consciousness of society, its essential soul, the expression of all nature.

The Third Millennium Revolution continues:

On the other hand, one cannot imagine that the amortization of the world can be constructed from a purely ethical perspective -- which could be accused of alienating or alienating.

In fact, the concepts and instruments in favour of the humanized society must also inspire, in addition to operational instruments, legal instruments appropriate to the organization of the new society, instruments that must necessarily be based on essential ethics and thus make it a criterion of its organization.

Ethics, thus understood as the appropriate conformation of behaviours or structures of social organization to the nature of the human being and his relationships (for this reason essential), constitutes more than ever an imposition for the survival of the process in this complex world that has reached human evolution. Consistent ethics, because it is essential, different from morality or moralism, the fruit of ideologies, habits and customs or the fashions of the time and place, and sometimes even the instrument of reducing the human dimensions, simply to base oneself on prejudices.

It is for this complex reality, for these demands or aspirations of human beings, which are sometimes diffuse, contradictory or even erroneous, that it is necessary to seek adequate responses, inserting into institutions the new values, those which make the new society possible, the values of post-technological civilization.

This is the essential dimension of the revolution of the third millennium.

The content of law in the post-technological era.

The Third Millennium Revolution continues to offer a new legal perspective, based on a line of law, appropriate to the technological revolution and its effects, and in line with the humanized society. This new law should constitute the way in which social values, the foundations of the new society, and its operational instruments, i.e. the essential ethics and its evolution, are transformed into legal norms, laws and institutions, characterizing the new organization of society and its functioning.

"If values and ethics evolve, and if they evolve in a manner consistent with their nature, one of the necessary characteristics of the new law -- the new legal norms -- lies in its ability to insert continuously and dynamically into institutions and behaviours the essential values or ethics so that the values and norms that govern them do not simply change in response to technological change or the conditioning it imposes, or the interests of those who control the system.

The new law, therefore, appropriate to the post-technological reality and committed to the ethical evolution of society, its institutions and behaviour, must aim to make institutions and procedures continuously appropriate to the nature of the process and its component parts: man and society.

This perspective implies a conceptual and, above all, practical revision of so-called positive law, so that it is no longer essentially an instrument for stratifying values, habits and customs, but rather an instrument for organizing processes of change or transformation. This is so that the essential ethics can be maintained and the ways to build a society that is truly human, minimally harmonious and therefore sustainable can be sought. According to the importance and speed that the social process assumes, the new law must be equipped with sufficient capacity to order new things and define the lines and limits of these things and their relationships. With this, it will reorganize the results of change, so that organization and human relations occur as an expression of the nature of things and its continuously changing process. It is necessary to conceive of law as constantly evolving, ordering reality, because reality itself -- reality, is constantly evolving. If this new law cannot be created, the opposition between law and reality, or the nature of things, will constitute an additional instrument in favour of rupture.

This means that the foundations of post-technological social organisation, deconcentration and cooperation, and the resulting rights to participation and the duty of solidarity, must be transformed into organising legal principles for the process of civilisation transition we are experiencing and for the new society resulting from this process.

Legal content of participation and solidarity.

The transformation of ethical principles into legal principles allows some final considerations on the question of solidarity (the ethical element of cooperation) and participation (the ethical element of deconcentration).

With regard to the concept of solidarity, a parallel can be drawn between what is happening today and what, in distant times, took place in relation to the concept of justice. Justice was a precept related more to virtue than to law or the law.

The citizen did not have to be fair. The strongest could oppress, enslave, and even kill the weakest. The codes, in general, admitted what would now be inadmissible: the law and the right of the strongest taking precedence over the weakest, that is, over the notion of justice.

In this conception, justice was a virtue, and the righteous man was recognized as virtuous, respected for it -- to be virtuous, by his community.

This conception of justice then equates, in a way, to the conception we have today of solidarity. Solidarity, rather than an object of the law, is considered a simple virtue. The law does not oblige anyone to be in solidarity, even if sometimes decisions invoke the duty of solidarity as a requirement inherent in the fullness of justice.

It is not enough, however, that the citizen in solidarity, as once the just, should be considered virtuous and worthy of praise for his virtue.

Solidarity must be imposed as a legal norm, involving the relationships of people, organizations and countries, because, in the conquests of the absolute power of technology, capable of concentrating everything, only solidarity will make it possible to achieve justice.

Globalization, interdependence, the immense distance that separates those who hold wealth, and therefore power and technology, from the legions of the excluded, imposes this progress on the institutions, legal, to allow the minimally balanced and therefore sustainable society.

Similar considerations can be applied to the concept of participation, the ethical counterpart of devolution.

Since participation is a universal right, it must, like solidarity, in addition to inspiring operational mechanisms, be transformed into legal norms that guarantee its exercise, i.e. universal access to participation must be ensured. Not only is ownership, whether of goods, power or knowledge, a right, but also being a right to participation, it is necessary that this principle, in its broad outline already recognized as a social right, has consequences, even if it affects the right to property, which may have to be limited, according to the right to participation, whenever such limitation is necessary.

The universality of participation refers to all elements of society, the people who make it up, and the different dimensions of life in society. It is not only a question of participation in income or material goods; it is also a question of access to cultural goods, political participation, coexistence relations, quality of life and, finally, all the dimensions that make up man and his circumstances, as expressed by Ortega y Gasset.

This includes, in particular, the right to participate in the progress of technology -- over which the principle of its social function as an essential instrument for promoting the participation of populations in the processes must also prevail.

The same right to participation of individuals extends to groups and countries, so that the balance is restored at the global level in society.

On the other hand, and in return, there is a need to extend and strengthen legal norms, at national and international level, against concentration mechanisms.
The current legislation relatively represses monopolies and other similar procedures. That is very little. It is not just a question of ensuring a certain competition between those who are more strongly in the market, according to the principles of liberalism or the free market, a kind of guarantee of interests. It is, in fact, a question of ensuring universal participation, a principle that goes far beyond guarantccing market competition.

This is the other dimension of the revolution, which remains to be done to make possible the new civilization, the civilization of the post-technological era.

3 – THE PATH OF ENCOURAGE OF LOVE[25].

Deconcentration and participation; cooperation and solidarity; participation and solidarity creating harmony and sustainability -- security and peace.

In the same way that deconcentration finds its ethical component in participation, and cooperation finds its ethical component in solidarity, participation and solidarity constitute the factors of harmony and balance in society and, consequently, the sustainability of security and peace, i.e. the path for the civilization of amorization. Harmony and peace of each person with himself, in the relationship between persons, the relationship between peoples and nations.

Is that possible?

This is not only possible, but inevitable, because this is the way that explains the harmony of the universe and nature, and therefore, also the path of human evolution. This, of course, will not be interrupted by those who deny or ignore its nature and its process conditioned by values and concepts earlier stages of the same process, this long and sometimes difficult ascent.

They have not been able to free themselves from the traditional packaging resulting from the pre-technological era, with its essential errors - "homo oeconomicus" or "homo hominis lupus." This reductive conception, trying to survive, is expressed in the theories of profit, accumulation and concentration without limits, erecting factors such as the essence of nature and the purpose of man, the determinants of sustainable organization, and human activities. Such a conception is no longer compatible, nor sustainable, with the post-technological era, where man has become capable of dominating nature, and destroying it, or has become capable of dominating other men and destroying them, becoming the new scourge of humanity. On the other hand, with the same means, and with the appropriate use of technology, he will also be able to build a new civilization and

---

[25] The word 'amorização' was coined in the 1950s by French anthropologist Teilhard Chardin, a Jesuit who dedicated his life to anthropological research in Africa and China. Because there is no similar term in the English language and in the greater degree of clarity of the concepts presented in this text, it translates 'amorização' (in French 'amortization' in Portuguese 'amorização') through the expression: 'encourage love' – which in a broad way means: encouragement to the civilization of love.

promote the realization, the full human realization, the continuity of the process of civilization and human evolution.

To this end, the same technology enables man to control nature, not to destroy it, but to transform it into a partner in its processes, just as it also enables the processes of competition, concentration and exclusion to be replaced by cooperation, by the multiplication of alternatives and by deconcentration, generating participation and solidarity, and thus pluralism and freedom, the vocation of man, as is evident from the anthropological vision proposed.

It will happen because that is the meaning of human evolution. When and how it will happen, or what price mankind will have to pay to reach this stage, will depend on the strength of resistance to transformation or, from another point of view, on man's capacity for change.

It is in this sense that we can understand Teilhard de Chardin's expression, already quoted, referring to love as the fabric that underlies the whole of nature and its evolutionary process. To build society -- the parcel that is part of nature, according to this fabric -- means to cushion the world.

Why can't love sustain man, his structures, relationships and attitudes and organize society as its essential element, if it is "love that moves the sun and all the stars"? I site Dante Alighieri, once again, because the poet has realized and expressed in its own way, an absolutely scientific truth, considering love, as we consider it, the complementarity and attraction between all beings, the complementarity and attraction which, in inanimate beings, can be called gravity or gravitation, and which, in the life of animals, can be called organic reaction, or instinct, but which takes on the dimension of love only in man, because of consciousness or freedom.

Just as it is not possible to remove the gravitation of celestial bodies and the gravity of all bodies, just as it is not possible to remove from living beings their organic systems and the instinct that preserves them, so it is not possible to remove from men and their relationships, love -- the love that moves the sun and the stars, without paying the equivalent price for this essential error.

The same absolute sense of love is found in Jesus Christ, to teach that "**love sums up all the law and the prophets**". We must consider that Jesus Christ created a civilization in the world based on love, and there are 2 billion Christians, his disciples, in addition to so many other followers of other guides or enlightened people of the human species who, by other means, and each in his own way, have the same intuition and teach the same vision of the world and of mankind ; forms, finally, as also perceived by the mystics of all currents, the metaphysicists and, increasingly, the scientists in the field of physics, nature and man, in their quest for an understanding of man in his essence, of the universe and of his circumstances.

This perception takes place more and more intensely in the field of intuition, philosophy and experimental science.

Why is it that only those who drive the driving systems, the case of "practical" experts and specialists who see the world as small, the size of their vision or their interests, they can only see the world in a simplistic way, unable to make it operational in accordance with its nature and wholeness, and just able to work according to concentration and exclusion, leading to disharmony, imbalance and unsustainability? Fulton J. Sheen, Bishop of New York in the 1950s of the last century, already understood that the microcosm -- the world of men -- was only a reflection of the macrocosm[26] and vice versa.

Universal gravitation, gravity, nature's cycles and systems, everything works by attraction and complementarity, whether mechanical, biological or instinctive. Why can't the human world function through cooperation, participation, solidarity and love, which are simply the conscious form of attraction and complementarity?

However, because no finished thing is perfect, this balance or harmony (or peace), can be broken, and nature pays high prices every time it breaks it. Because of freedom, or its misuse, this fracture can affect men much and more severely than the way other things in nature are affected.

Thus, the functioning of human organizations, as part of this finiteness, will never be perfect, and there will be ruptures. Like nature, of which it is a part, man will pay the price for the ruptures he makes, or allows to be made. But the organization, the structure and the essence of the process, cannot be constructed by rupture factors. The price of this error can be absolute, in the dimension of the

---

[26]Sheen J. Fulton - O Mistério do Amor - Agir Editor - 1955.

technology of the new era, if man is not capable of understanding and constructing himself, his circumstances and his environment -- nature, of which he is a part.

Because of the misuse of freedom, confused with disordered complexity -- chaos, man has moved away from men more than he has moved away from himself, eventually, nature is pre-determined in its processes. Any contrary effect refers to the orderly approach to complexity -- harmony.

To amortize the world or society means to bring man and human organization back into harmony with the universe, integrated within himself and with other men.

This distance, if not reversed, with the speed of the process and globalisation, that is to say the absolute dimension of technology, threatens to lead the process to a certain kind of rupture, much more serious than any other rupture that has taken place in the past and for which man will be able to pay a very high price, perhaps as the dinosaurs paid millions of years ago in a cosmic cataclysm that eliminated them from history.

However, freedom exists in man because of conscience, and conscience allows the use of freedom to minimize errors and distortions, not to exacerbate them. It also makes it possible to retrace the road and get back on track. This is the space of freedom, as a stage in the evolution of civilization in which the bonds of love must be strengthened and must support and move people, society and nations in an invisible and **sustainable way -- the fabric of the universe "moves the sun and all the stars".**

Some must consider this proposal confused because it mixes the micro and the macro, because it receives a vision that can be considered by both, mystical (intuitive), philosophical (metaphysical) or practical (or experimental) and this has already been commented on.

But isn't nature multiple in its parts and holistic in its entirety? Why is it that only the vision of man and society cannot be multiple and holistic, but must always be reductive, simplifying the complex things that constitute it?

The official science or segmentation of reality, as a method of analysis, is legitimate. When, however, the method becomes reality, deforming it, dividing what is indivisible (except as a method), monsters and monstrosities of all kinds end up being created. This is what those who reject or ignore the **global, holistic, or essential** vision of **reality** do.

There will be resistance to this approach, because it is different from the world and from the perspective of being and coexisting human beings. It is seen as the essence, the nature, and focuses on the future and not on the past, although it considers the past as a cause, or a process. Society has paid, and still pays, and will pay a much higher price if it does not does not understand nature, process and cause, and that it continues to resist change, or evolution in its dimension of civilizational leap.

However, this leap is the vocation of the human species. It is a particularly strong and urgent vocation at this threshold of the new era that is imposed as a consequence of the technological leap and the moment when the history of human evolution arrived.

Finally, it must be understood that the participatory and supportive society, or the loving world -- the post-technological civilization -- is not a point of arrival, the final point of the process, but only one more step on the path that will lead man and the world around him, like an arrow launched from the Alpha point to the Omega point, to the fullness of its realization.

LETTER FOR A PARTICIPATIVE AND UNITED CIVILIZATION

This letter was presented to the Permanent Forum of Participation and Solidarity, promoted by the UNISUL Chair of Participation and Solidarity, created by the Universidad del Sur de Santa Catarina, Brazil.

Osvaldo Della Giustina - Boss

The crises that have worried and anguished mankind since the beginning of the millennium go beyond a simple financial crisis, as it seems, and are generally interpreted. They are, above all, the consequence of dysrhythmias resulting from the imbalances introduced into the process of civilization, between the speed of technological evolution and its use, and the slowness with which changes in people and institutions are taking place. Such dysrhythmia produces imbalances. These imbalances affect society in each of its elements, people in all their dimensions, and the nature, home and dwelling of mankind.

Yet there is no opposition between technology and its advances and man in his multiple dimensions, even considering technology in its most advanced forms, such as genetic engineering, fine chemistry, or cosmic physics.

Opposition, therefore, exists when technology advances or is used according to man and society, its rhythms, its values and the environment where human phenomena occur. On the contrary, technology can become a powerful instrument to press the rhythms of improvement of people and institutions towards a new stage of civilization. However, as dysrhythmia and the imbalances it causes persist, a succession of crises will be inevitable and their aggravation may lead the process to some form of rupture, of unimaginable dimensions and consequences.

But the path of breaking up is not a necessary path. Parallel to this threat and the slow evolution of men and their institutions, a powerful mass of consciousness is growing in the world in defence of man, his values and the acceleration of the pace of his own change and the change of institutions.

Constituting the essential mass content of consciousness for human dignity and its fundamental rights, among them, above all, the right to life and to equal opportunities of access to the goods necessary for a fulfilled life. This process must be extended to all human beings, whatever their colour, race, culture, beliefs, social category, or any attribute. Pluralism of cultures, thought, political systems, beliefs or morals are presuppositions for the exercise of human dignity and freedom, as well as for the harmonious coexistence, peace and self-confidence of peoples and nations, the fruit of participation and solidarity. These and other elements which constitute the very essence of the mass of consciousness find their synthesis in these values of ethical dimension.

It is necessary and urgent that these values -- participation and solidarity -- be assumed, individually by people and, collectively, by societies and nations, as viable presuppositions and foundations of the new human-scale society at this time of civilizational transition from the past to the post-technological era.

This perspective is not, however, a mere ethical duty. It relates to the very survival of the human being and his or her environment. The dimension of technology capable of destroying the world, not only physically, but in all its dimensions no longer allows the permanence of paradigms of the past, based on conflict, wild competition to the point of unlimited concentration, finally, in the field and use of technology as an instrument of social exclusion, dangerously unbalancing the civilizational process.

Consensus has to be built while ethical values, participation and solidarity make us dream of new utopias, but also compel and inspire new practical formulations capable of guiding the transition of civilization and ordering the post-technological society.

According to this understanding, participation and solidarity must, and can, be transformed into instruments capable of recreating man and new institutions by rebalancing the process of civilization and overcoming crises and the threat of breakdown. This means hastening the arrival of the evolved, united and participatory human being and raising political, economic and social systems in all their elements to a new stage of human coexistence.

That is why it is necessary to perceive, and to assume, that participation, as an ethical value, finds in the deconcentration of all human and social dimensions an effective instrument for change. Deconcentration causes an overcoming of the concentrating systems, more powerful in this era of globalization and more harmful, through competition that excludes and the unlimited occupation of space, to produce the exclusion of persons, regions, peoples and nations. This exclusion takes place in the growing process that will soon arrive, at this critical moment, or the rupture, in case it is not reversible.

It must be perceived, and also assumed, that solidarity as an ethical value finds in cooperation, instead of limitless competition and unlimited occupation of space, producing exclusion, an appropriate instrument for rebalancing society, organizing it in a sustainable way towards the new post-technological era.

A better world is possible

This invitation to build a better, participatory and united world is addressed in particular to universities, social organizations, governments and political leaders, as well as other segments of society, the media, promoters of art, intelligence and culture, and also churches and philosophies of all kinds, to focus on the moment and the process, promoting an in-depth, rigorous and effective analysis of what is happening in the world and its uncertainties linked to the succession of crises, and to formulate systematized and operational proposals to overcome/reverse the process of rupture that threatens us. In this way, the values of the mass of consciousness will actually make the world a better place, more united, more participatory, more humane and more adapted to the progress of science and technology.

UNISUL Chair Participation and Solidarity
Tubarão, Santa Catarina,
18 May 2009.

Table of Contents